Northern Lighthouses

"Jones and Roberts have unerringly captured the fascination and mystery of . . . these lovely, wind-swept beacons. . . . Dramatic histories are complemented by an array of breathtaking . . . photographs. . . . Will pique the curiosity . . . of people who didn't even know they were interested in lighthouses."

—BOOKPAGE

"Beautifully photographed . . . each profile includes . . . a history of the light and its former keepers and directions to the site."

—SUNDAY CAPE COD TIMES

"A coastal sightseeing guide . . . more than 70 photos accompany the lighthouses' histories."

—SOUNDINGS

"Lighthouse fans will get their money's worth . . . the uninitiated will discover a world of fascinating lore. The stories are lessons in American history, whimsy, and derring-do, and the color photographs are artistic vignettes that stand on their own."

—COLONIAL HOMES

by Bruce Roberts and Ray Jones

SOUTHERN LIGHTHOUSES
Chesapeake Bay to the Gulf of Mexico

WESTERN LIGHTHOUSES
Olympic Peninsula to San Diego

GREAT LAKES LIGHTHOUSES
Ontario to Superior

AMERICAN COUNTRY STORES

STEEL SHIPS AND IRON MEN
*A Tribute to World War II Fighting Ships
and the Men Who Served on Them*

NORTHERN LIGHTHOUSES

New Brunswick to the Jersey Shore

SECOND EDITION

Photographs by Bruce Roberts
Text by Ray Jones

A Voyager Book

The
Globe
Pequot
Press

Old Saybrook, Connecticut

ACKNOWLEDGMENTS

We sincerely appreciate the assistance of Coast Guard historians Robert L. Scheina, Dr. Robert Browning, Kenneth Arbogast, and other men and women of the U.S. Coast Guard; Ken Black of the Shore Village Museum in Rockport, Maine; Wayne Wheeler of the United States Lighthouse Society; William L. Trotter of the American Lighthouse Historical Society; Tim Harrison of *Lighthouse Digest*; Bill Kaufhold for his excellent photographs; Cliff Benfield of Horton Point Lighthouse, Long Island, New York; Ben and Luanne Russell of Hendricks Head Lighthouse, Maine; The Rose Island Lighthouse Foundation, Rhode Island; Tom Laverty of Navesink Lighthouse, New Jersey; and Candace Clifford of the National Park Service Maritime Initiative, Washington, D.C.

Library of Congress Cataloging-in-Publication Data
Roberts, Bruce.
    Northern lighthouses : New Brunswick to the Jersey Shore / photographs by Bruce Roberts :
text by Ray Jones — 2nd ed.
      p. cm.
    "A Voyager Book."
    Includes bibliographical references and index.
    ISBN 1–56440-406-4
    1. Lighthouses—New England. 2. Lighthouses—Middle Atlantic States. 3. New England—History, Local. 4. Middle Atlantic States—History, Local. I. Jones, Ray. II. Title.
VK1024N38R63 1994
387.1'55'0974—dc20   93–45635
                                                                           CIP

Cover photographs: front, Portland Head Light, Portland, Maine; back, Highland Light, Cape Cod, Massachusetts
Cover and text design by Nancy Freeborn

Manufactured in Hong Kong by Everbest Printing Co., Ltd. through Four Color Imports, Ltd.
Second Edition/First Printing

To my daughter Lori —*Bruce Roberts*

To George Worthylake, Ida Lewis, and Dennis Dever —*Ray Jones*

With its classic lighthouse and romantic setting, Pemaquid Point reminds visitors of their intimate link to the sea.

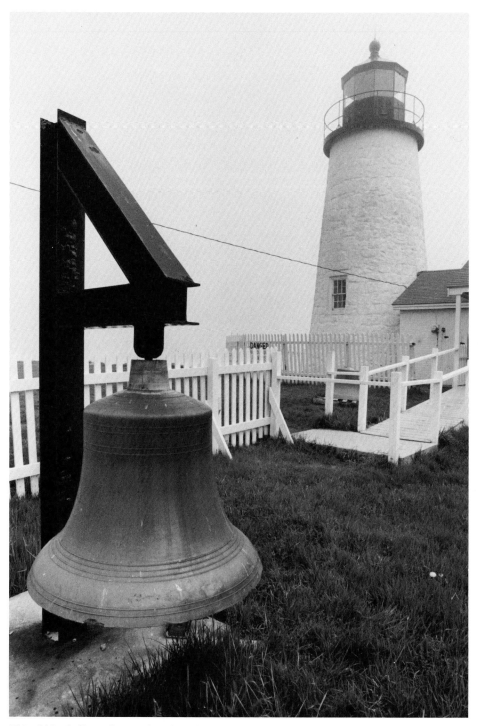

This old fog bell saved many ships from disaster off Pemaquid Point.

CONTENTS

INTRODUCTION

"No man is an island." So said John Donne, the often-quoted British poet and clergyman. But Donne, who died in 1631, never knew any of the lighthouse keepers who, for more than two centuries, helped make America's coasts safe for navigation. For these brave men and women, life was an island. Surviving on subsistence-level government salaries, they lived mostly on wild headlands and treeless ledges very far from what most of us would call civilization. Often the closest town was itself a backwater, a remote outpost. Depending on the weather, even the nearest rural church might seem impossibly distant.

When bad weather rushed in from the ocean, as it often did, lighthouse keepers could not follow the example of the mariners they served and run for a calm harbor. Since their ships had stone foundations and no sails, rudders, or helms, they had to stay and take whatever the sea threw at them. To fight back against gale and gloom, they had only their lights, and whatever the conditions, whatever the health of the keepers, these had to be kept burning. The lamps, which often stood at the top of winding staircases with hundreds of steps, were in constant need of attention. As a result, the keepers always worked nights and rarely had a day off.

Lighthouse keepers endured this sort of existence, not necessarily for any high-minded or romantic reason—for instance, because they loved the sea, the wind, the cold, or the isolation—but for the same reason that most people work: It rewarded them with a place to live and a smattering of pay. It was also a job worth doing, a job that had to be done.

RIVERS IN THE SEA

The waters just off the East Coast of the United States serve as a superhighway for ships. Two great rivers in the Atlantic, the cold Labrador Current flowing down from the north and the warm Gulf Stream sweeping up from the south, form the separate lanes of this highway. For centuries, all the way back to the time of the earliest explorers, mariners have used these swift-flowing currents to speed their ships back and forth from Europe.

Because the currents hug the coast, ships sailing in these natural sea lanes are constantly at risk of running aground on shoals or smacking into some fog-shrouded headland. Sometimes ships slip into the wrong lane, where they may collide with another vessel sailing in the opposite direction. As a consequence of these dangers, the sandy sea bottom along the North American East Coast has become a graveyard covered with the ribs of wrecked ships and the bones of unlucky seamen.

For at least two centuries lighthouses have served as the "traffic cops" of this crowded and dangerous ocean highway, warning ships away from knife-edged rocks and guiding them safely to port. Dozens of lightships also once provided guidance, but all of these have now been pulled off station and retired. According to the Coast Guard, which maintains lighthouses, buoys, and other aids to navigation in U.S. waters, the old lightships have simply outlived their usefulness.

But lighthouses remain vital to shipping, especially along the bustling U.S. eastern seaboard. The beacons of nearly 200 lighthouses form an almost continuous band of light along the thousands of miles of coastline between Brownsville, Texas, on the U.S.-Mexican border, and West Quoddy Head, Maine, just across a narrow channel from Canada. More than half of the total are located north of the famed Mason-Dixon Line. The more historic and picturesque of these "northern lights" are the subjects of this book. So, too, are the brave men and women who have kept the lights burning through the centuries.

BOSTON LIGHTS THE WAY

The first true lighthouse in North America was built on Little Brewster Island at the entrance to Boston Harbor. George Worthylake, a shepherd and harbor pilot, climbed to the top of the newly completed tower on the evening of September 14, 1716. There, with the sun descending in the west and a blanket of darkness racing across the ocean from the east, Worthylake put a match to the light's tallow candles for the first time. On that night and the many thousands of nights since, the masters of ships headed for Boston have seen the light and known that safe water lay ahead. Mariners still see it today, more than 270 years after Worthylake first climbed the tower steps.

After the light on Little Brewster was established, Boston became a magnet to shipping, and merchants and warehousemen along the city's waterfront prospered. The new lighthouse proved far less profitable for Worthylake, however. Fate had no fortune in store for him. His salary of fifty pounds a year was supposed to be supplemented by fees for serving as harbor pilot. But Worthylake's responsibilities as keeper proved much more arduous and time-consuming than expected, and he had little time left over for piloting.

To help feed and clothe his family, the keeper ran herds of sheep on Little Brewster and other nearby islands, but Worthylake had no more luck as a

This illustration from a nineteenth-century Lighthouse Service publication shows a second-order Fresnel lens.

shepherd than he did as a pilot. During a terrible winter gale in 1717, several dozen of his sheep wandered out onto a spit, where they were soon stranded by the tide. Since he could not in good conscience abandon his post in the midst of a storm, Worthylake could do nothing to assist these hapless animals. From the high lantern room of the lighthouse he watched in despair as one after another of his sheep washed off the spit and into the sea.

In all, Worthylake lost fifty-nine sheep to the storm. To help ease the financial burden of this loss, the town of Boston agreed to increase the keeper's salary to seventy pounds. Unfortunately, Worthylake never got to enjoy his new salary. As he was returning from Boston, where he had gone to collect his pay, his boat capsized only a hundred yards or so from the safety of the dock on Little Brewster Island. The shepherd-turned-lighthouse keeper drowned, and his body washed ashore on the same spit where his sheep had perished. By the time his body was discovered, the money he had received in Boston had mysteriously vanished.

Robert Saunders, the second Boston keeper, also drowned only a few days after he took over the job. But, undaunted by the misfortunes of his predecessors, Captain John Hayes replaced Saunders, and the new American profession of lighthouse keeping lived on. Hayes and most of the nearly sixty keepers who followed him to Little Brewster survived their stay on the island even if they did not always prosper there.

The profession in itself, however, will not survive forever. After more than two-and-a-half centuries, it is apparently dying of old age. Technology has replaced the sure eyes and steady hands of lighthouse keepers with radio-monitored relays and automatic timers. Having repeatedly drawn the short straw in annual federal budget cuts, the Coast Guard can no longer afford to staff its light stations. Given responsibility for the nation's lighthouses and other navigational aids in 1939, the frugal Coast Guard automated one light after another. Often, the old keeper's dwellings were auctioned off, converted to other uses, or allowed to fall into a sad state of disrepair.

Ironically, the last lighthouse in America to be looked after by a regular Coast Guard keeper is the Boston Light; it, too, may soon be unmanned and automated. Today, except for the Boston Light, America's eastern lighthouses stand alone. Computers and other automated equipment have replaced the skilled keepers, however, and the lights continue their necessary work of marking the nation's coasts.

AMERICA'S LAST KEEPER

Coast Guardsman Dennis Dever, one of the last men to serve as keeper of the Boston Light, is very good with his hands. Boaters in Boston's outer harbor often think they have seen Dever when, in fact, they have not. Like the swarms of less-than-clever seagulls that suspiciously eye the concrete light-station dock from a distance, the boaters are fooled by Dever's scarecrow, which wears an official Coast Guard uniform and bears a fleeting resemblance to the keeper himself. Dever hates the mess the gulls make on the concrete, so he built the scarecrow in the station woodshop. Using a wooden float, he also made a large owl that spins around in the wind and scowls menacingly at the gulls.

"I learned to do a lot of stuff out here that I would never have thought twice about on the mainland," said Dever.

For instance, Dever, who said he had never before put his hand to a hoe, has become an avid gardener on Little Brewster. He grows handsome JFK roses, not to mention turnips, tomatoes, cucumbers, cabbages, pumpkins, and a variety of other vegetables. Keepers once had to garden in order to put food on their tables, but Dever does it just for fun and to keep his hands busy when there is no work to do on the light.

At first a tribe of voracious island rats savaged Dever's crops, but the keeper imported a black cat. Like the gulls, the rats soon learned to keep their distance. Steeped in the lore of lighthouses, Dever named his cat Ida Lewis, after the heroine and keeper of the Lyme Rock Light in Newport, Rhode Island.

Dever grew up hearing stories about lighthouses and extraordinary people like Ida Lewis. His father was a keeper who tended lights at Egg Rock, Bass Harbor, Bakers Island, and Great Duck Island, all in Maine. With a background like that, it would seem Dever is a good choice to serve as one of America's last lighthouse keepers.

"Since my father was a keeper, it was always in the back of my mind that, someday, I might be, too," said Dever. "But, of course, I never thought I would be the last."

Of course, Coast Guards-men continue to operate the automated lights, but they do so from a distance. Using electronic controls and radio transmitters to monitor performance, they pay only sporadic visits to the lonely towers themselves. On the other hand, at Little Brewster, Dever's daily routine is not so different from the one George Worthylake followed in 1716. In addition to tending the light, he looks after the station buildings and keeps an eye out for mariners in distress.

As with countless keepers before him, one of Dever's most important duties is the daily cleaning and polishing of the big lens in the lantern room. Made in Paris about 130 years ago, it is a classic Fresnel lens with 336 separate prisms and twelve bull's-eyes. By 1860 the government fitted American lighthouses with Fresnel lenses. These gathered up light from a whale oil, lard oil, kerosene, or, in

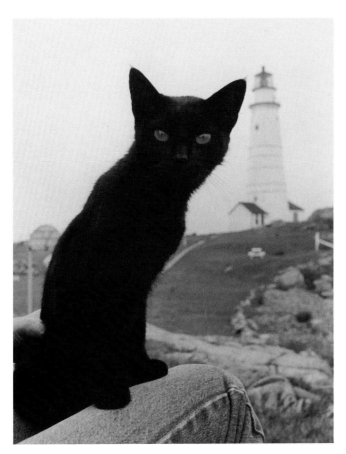

Ida Lewis, a whiskered denizen of the Boston Light station, takes advantage of a friendly lap. She is named for the heroine and keeper of Lime Rock Lighthouse in Newport, Rhode Island.

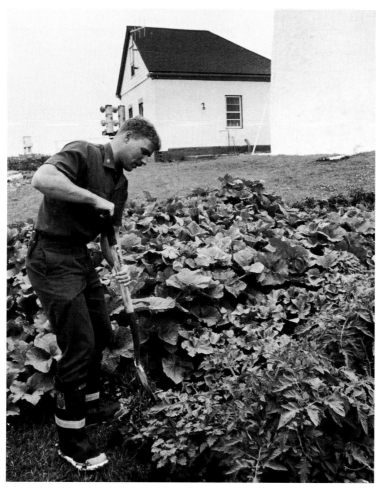

Dennis Dever says he never put his hand to a hoe before he became a lighthouse keeper, but here on Little Brewster Island he grows cabbages and pumpkins of impressive size. Ida Lewis helps by keeping rats out of the garden.

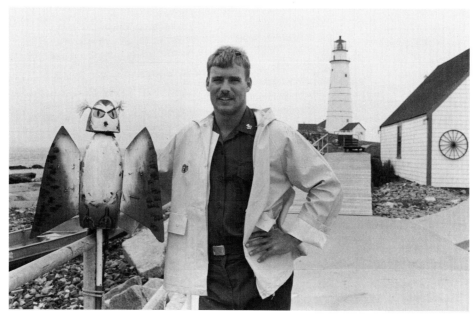

To make the seagulls think twice about using the station's concrete dock as a bombing range—making a general nuisance of themselves—Dever fashioned this spinning owl from a wooden lobster float.

this century, electric lamp and concentrated it into a tightly focused beam that could often be seen from dozens of miles away. The lenses came in a variety of sizes or "orders." The sixth-order lenses were only seventeen inches high with an inside diameter of less than a foot, while the huge first-order lenses stood nearly eight feet tall and had a diameter of more than six feet.

The Boston Light has a second-order Fresnel lens about fourteen feet tall and sixty-six inches in diameter. As any other professional keeper would have done, Dever treats the old lens with enormous respect. "It has been here a while longer than I have," he said. "If anybody moves this thing or breaks it, it's going to be an [Coast Guard] officer and not me."

Dever celebrated his twenty-ninth birthday in 1989; that same year the Boston lens reached the age of 130, and the light station itself entered its 273rd year of service. Numbers like those might seem overwhelming to some young people, but not to Dever. He regards the rich history of the Boston Light with a curious combination of awe and good humor. A questionable liquid, apparently brewed with some regularity in the kitchen of the station residence, is labeled "George Worthylake Mead."

A sense of humor, and perhaps a touch or two of the mead, make it at least a little easier for young Dever to weather the winter gales that shake the island and send Ida Lewis scurrying under the table. In any case, he does weather them. No more and certainly no less dedicated than the thousands of American lighthouse keepers who came before him, Dever grits his teeth, keeps a close eye on his light, and waits out the storm.

A BELL IN THE NIGHT

Several miles south of the Boston Light, Minots Ledge Lighthouse stands on a scrap of rock that disappears under the waves at each high tide. The tower usually cannot be made out from Little Brewster, but at night, unless the weather is especially heavy, its light can always be seen. The granite Minots tower is the second lighthouse built on the ledge. The first was an experimental structure, an iron skeleton with eight legs that stood with their feet in the ocean. In a raging storm in the early morning darkness of March 17, 1851, the experiment failed.

When the gale had set in the previous night, keeper John Bennett was on the mainland. The weather was so severe, the keeper could not return to his post. This left the light in the hands of assistant keepers Joseph Antoine and Joseph Wilson, both close friends of Bennett. As the storm grew worse and titanic waves began to roll in out of the east, Bennett and other spectators on shore began to wonder if the lighthouse could possibly stand up to the pounding. Their fears were well founded.

Shortly after one o'clock, the skeleton began to sag toward land. The tearful Bennett, who realized now that he would never again speak to his two friends, noted with bitter pride that somehow his assistants kept the light burning right down to the last instant. As the lantern room neared the water, just before the lighthouse collapsed and fell into the sea, the waves began to hit the station fog bell, causing it to ring out wildly.

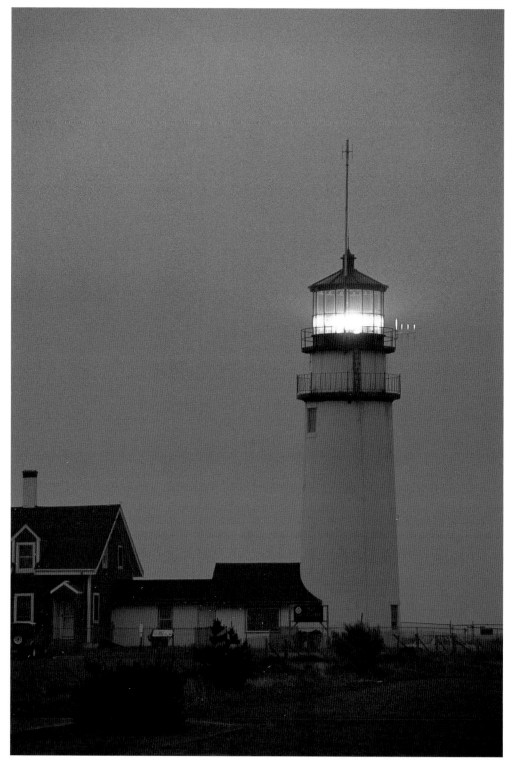

Highland Light dominates a high, sandy bluff on famed Cape Cod. Among the oldest light stations in the United States, it was established in 1798, while George Washington was still president.

CHAPTER ONE

LIGHTS
WAY DOWN EAST

Northern Coast of Maine

Lights Way Down East

CANADA

MAINE

East Quoddy Head

West Quoddy Head

• Bangor

Fort Point

Ellsworth •

Dice Head

Prospect Harbor Point

Egg Rock

Eagle Island

Bass Harbor Head

Burnt Coat Harbor

Great Duck Island

Isle au Haut

Baker Island

Saddleback Ledge

Mount Desert Rock

Matinicus Rock

Atlantic Ocean

Isolation breeds eloquence. For proof of this one only need turn to the logs and letters of America's lighthouse keepers. As members of a profession that paid them barely enough to live, these rugged, rawboned men and women were frugal in all things, even in their use of language. Nature and circumstance taught them to place a special value on words. Huddled together on roadless headlands or barren ledges far out in the sea, the keepers and their families soon ran out of small talk. They spoke only when they needed to speak, and even then, they whittled their sentences down to an efficient minimum. A thing had to be said and done with; otherwise, the words blew away in the wind or drowned in the roar of the ocean.

Even so, some have counted lighthouse keepers among the world's best storytellers. Wordsmiths the likes of Daniel Webster and Henry David Thoreau have smoked pipes and sipped mugs of coffee with New England keepers and felt tingles running up their spines at stories of storm, shipwreck, sacrifice, and heroism. Thoreau especially admired the keeper's way of spinning a tale, not with miles of silk but with a few yards of good, stout yarn.

Today, the Down East portion of Maine is still considered out-of-the-way. Imagine how it seemed a century ago to lighthouse keepers who lived on islands and cliff-top outposts distant even from the region's remote coastal towns and villages. What was it like to live in a Down East lighthouse? In the following passages, the keepers tell their own stories.

A REAL HUMMER

After the light itself, the chief concern of a lighthouse keeper was the weather. Probably no other profession ever exposed its members to worse in the way of climate. The keepers of island and ledge lights and caisson-style lighthouses built directly over the shoals they guarded were especially vulnerable to bad weather. In a gale a lighthouse, such as the one on Saddleback Ledge in Penobscot Bay, is a ship without a helm. Unable to run for a safe harbor, or duck into a quiet cove, it is a motionless obstacle standing directly in the path of a furious ocean.

Saddleback Ledge keeper W. W. Wells described one such angry sea to a fellow "Wickie," or lighthouse keeper:

"The storm struck in the dead of night, the wind blew a sixty-mile gale. With it came the seas. They struck plentiful and hard. I did not even dare to peek out the door to see what was doing. We had the shutters all closed on the windows so as not to break any glass. . . . One tremendous [sea that boarded us] seemed to shake us like a tablecloth. I thought it was going to

clean up the works. Why it didn't I have never been able to fathom out. When the storm subsided, we ventured out to look things over.

"Things were certainly a mess. Over 128 feet of our boat slip was torn up, sink spout ripped away, and the cement breakwater built around the light to protect it, broken through in several places. It trimmed up our boathouse doors that were very strongly made. It threw a 140-gallon oil tank and boathouse door upon the winch hoist and put that out of commission. . . . It ripped the slopboards off on the east side of the house, and water came in from the roof where it had torn off the shingles. Take it altogether, it was a hummer."

NIGHT OF THE BIRDS

When it came to weather, keepers learned to expect the unexpected. Usually they were prepared for gales that flew in off the ocean with little or no warning. But nature had other surprises in store—for instance, attacks by airborne armies of suicidal ducks. Wells told the following story to a friend:

"We keepers were setting in the kitchen talking about the [First] World War when bang, bang, bang, something came against the windowpanes. We thought that another war had started that we had not heard about.

"All at once I heard glass smash in the lantern, and with this I thought sure the enemy were trying to extinguish the light.

"This was just around supper time and it lasted until near midnight. Darkness had come on and with it came all the evidence that we were going to get a Sou'easter. As the storm struck so did the cannonading. I could not help thinking that it was only fair to inform us of the attack that was about to be made. A war with Mexico and Japan seemed to be the last topic of conversation just before the unexpected arrived. But who wanted to blow up a friendly old lighthouse that always did good instead of harm, and which mariners who sailed their ships along the coast loved and respected. Crash! and a bird came sailing through a pane of glass, dropping at my feet.

"He began fluttering around the floor with one wing broken, and his bill telescoped almost through his head. He did not live long. In came another and away went another windowpane. The phenomenon was repeated again and again until the birds began to pile up like a mound.

"Just when I thought the cannonading had ceased, one big sea drake struck the plate glass in the tower lantern and came through without asking for a transfer. When he struck he broke up the works. Before he stopped he put out the light and broke prisms out of the lens. The bird weighed over ten pounds.

"Saddleback in darkness, what would the people think on land and sea? Only those who live in lighthouses could realize what excitement it all caused. The keepers got right to work, first to get the light going and then to make repairs as fast as possible. It was not long before old Saddleback was throwing her beams again as if nothing had ever happened.

Lighthouse beacons may be white, green, or, like Bass Harbor Light shown above, red. As with traffic lights on streets and highways, a red lighthouse beacon signals danger. In addition to guiding vessels into nearby Bass Harbor, this light also warns sailors away from the ship-killing rocks of Mount Desert Island.

"One of us went to step out in the gallery when a big sea duck reported with bayonet and charged so heavily as to knock one's feet out from under. There was no more taking any chances leaving the kitchen until continued silence told the keepers that the enemy had retreated. When all had quieted down, it was a strange sight that the keepers were greeted with, for at the base of the tower was a tremendous heap of birds, some dead and others alive. Those that were just dazed and needed to recuperate we placed in the boathouse, and the next day they went on their way."

WRECK ON MOUNT DESERT ROCK

Lighthouse keepers less frequently played host to dazed ducks than to half-drowned seamen. Since they lived on the most dangerous stretches of coast, keepers often witnessed calamitous wrecks and nearly as often helped drag survivors out of the surf. For shipwrecked sailors, a keeper might serve as rescuer, physician, and innkeeper.

A keeper on Mount Desert Rock left the following record of the early twentieth-century wreck of the tug *Astral:*

"It was on December 9th, 1902 at 5 o'clock in the morning that the second assistant keeper whose morning watch it was, called me saying "I think I heard a steamboat blow a blast of seven whistles as if in distress."

"I jumped out of bed and dressed as quickly as possible. The vapor was flying so high and densely that one could see hardly ten feet ahead. It was inky dark and blowing one of the worst gales I had seen since being in the service.

"The thermometer never had dropped so low during the thirteen years I had been on the Rock. The assistant had noticed that the sounds of the whistle came from the northeast and so we went in that direction. It was then high tide but we could, after a fashion, make out that there was some kind of steamer ashore on the northeast point; but as the big seas were running so mountain high it would have meant suicide for any of us to try to get out where she was.

"The seas were running through between the main rock and the outer point. I could see that no boat could live to get to the outer point and across the expanse of rough water. We called and called, trying to get an answer. Not hearing or seeing anything, we stayed where we were until we nearly froze to death. We could not stand the terrific cold air and simply had to get back to the station. We were chilled to the bones and could hardly speak when we got into the house.

"My wife had plenty of boiling water and a big pot of coffee ready to serve instantly. As soon as we got thawed out so we could handle our fingers we began getting down ropes and life preservers as near the wreck as we could. We were compelled to wait until the tide went down and then we got across to the outer point. We could then see that it was a large ocean tug with a barge in tow. The terrific blows that the sea was pounding on the craft would turn her almost completely over. Between the seas I was able to get a line to them and, one by one, we succeeded in rescuing seventeen men.

"There were eighteen in the crew but one was frozen to death before we could get him ashore. They were all more or less frozen, and badly at that. The second engineer of the tug had to be carried to the house, his limbs being useless. He was in terrible condition. . . . Well, after we got them all to the house we treated their frostbites and got them a hot breakfast. That night we doused them with quinine pills and hot lemonade for fear they might come down with bad colds and pneumonia might set in."

THE WORST SEA IS COMING

The keepers were not the only ones who faced hardship, danger, and punishing weather. Their families usually shared in the heavy work of keeping the lights burning, more often than not displaying the same heroic resolve as the keepers themselves.

On a stormy night in 1856, young Abbie Burgess drew up a chair to the kitchen table at the battered keeper's residence on Matinicus Rock and dipped her pen into ink. A lonely seventeen-year-old, separated by at least twenty-five miles of turbulent sea from the nearest barn dance, church social, or country store, she had decided to write a letter to a pen pal on the mainland:

"You have often expressed a desire to view the sea out on the ocean when it was angry. Had you been here on 19 January [1856], I surmise you would have been satisfied. Father was away. Early in the day, as the tide rose, the sea made a complete breach over the rock, washing every movable thing away, and of the old dwelling not one stone was left upon another. The new dwelling was flooded, and the windows had to be secured to prevent the violence of the spray from breaking them in. As the tide came, the sea rose higher and higher, till the only endurable places were the light towers. If they stood, we were saved, otherwise our fate was only too certain. But for some reason, I know not why, I had no misgivings, and went on with my work as usual. For four weeks, owing to rough weather, no landing could be effected on the rock. During this time we were without assistance of any male member of our family. Though at times greatly exhausted with my labors, not once did the lights fail. I was able to perform all my accustomed duties as well as my father's.

"You know the hens are our only companions. Becoming convinced, as the gale increased, that unless they were brought into the house they would be lost, I said to mother, "I must try to save them." She advised me not to attempt it. The thought, however, of parting with them without an effort was not to be endured, so seizing a basket, I ran out a few yards after the rollers had passed and the sea fell off a little, with the water knee deep, to the coop, and rescued all but one. It was the work of a moment, and I was back in the house with the door fastened, but I was none too quick, for at that instant my little sister, standing at the window, exclaimed, "Oh look! look there! The worst sea is coming." That wave destroyed the old dwelling and swept the rock. I cannot think you would enjoy remaining here any great length of time for the sea is never still and when agitated, its roar shuts out every other sound, even drowning our voices."

A few years after the extraordinary monthlong Atlantic storm described in her letter, Abbie Burgess married a lighthouse keeper. She and her husband eventually became assistant keepers of the Matinicus Rock Light.

EAST QUODDY HEAD LIGHT
Campobello Island, New Brunswick, Canada

Franklin D. and Eleanor Roosevelt maintained a thirty-four-room "cottage" on Campobello Island, where they spent many pleasant summers. It is easy to imagine the Roosevelts scrambling over the rocks to picnic within sight of the huge red cross that distinguishes the East Quoddy Head Lighthouse tower. Such an outing would not have been possible, however, after Franklin Roosevelt was stricken with polio. His first symptoms appeared while he was on holiday with his family at Campobello. Some say Roosevelt may have contracted the dread disease while swimming in the nearby St. Johns River. Although crippled for life, Roosevelt went on to win election as governor of New York and to serve three full terms and part of a fourth term as president during a crucial period of U.S. history.

East Quoddy Head Light, also known as Head Harbor Light, is located at the northern end of Campobello Island in New Brunswick, Canada. It

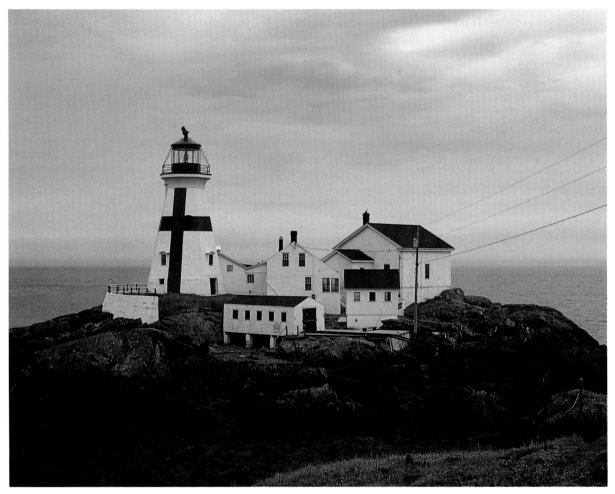

Displaying the red-cross design seen on many other Canadian lighthouses, East Quoddy Head Light station warns sailors away from this treacherous headland with a red beacon. Tides here can rise at the incredible rate of five feet per hour.

stands approximately sixteen miles from the Roosevelt cottage and about eighteen miles from the international bridge linking the island to Lubec, Maine. Like a flock of gulls perched on a rock beside the sea, the white tower and outbuildings cluster together on a rugged and barren headland

The buildings and much of the octagonal tower are of wood construction. The roofs of the buildings and the lantern atop the tower are all painted red. The large red cross on the side of the tower, a typical marking for Canadian lighthouses, is said to make the station easier to see when the headland is covered by snow. The lantern displays a fixed red light intended to warn ships away from the headland's jagged rocks.

To reach this unusually scenic light you must cross the international bridge at the end of Route 189 in Lubec. Customs officials there may suggest you register your camera equipment before entering Canada. Roughly two miles from the bridge you will pass the Roosevelt cottage, which is maintained by the Canadian government as the chief attraction of Roosevelt Park. If American history or the Roosevelt family interest you, then plan to spend an afternoon there. About a mile beyond the cottage, take a right at an unmarked intersection and continue for approximately fifteen miles. The last three miles of the road are dirt.

The lighthouse tower, outbuildings, and grounds are all closed to the public and are difficult to see from the parking area. But you can get an excellent view by climbing down an iron ladder, crossing a gray pebble beach, and then climbing up another metal ladder to the summit of the cliff on the opposite side. Beware~! The rungs of the ladders are very slippery, as are the algae-covered rocks below them. Unless you are cautious and surefooted, you may end up on a stretcher. Also, keep a close eye on the water level. The tides here rise at the incredible rate of five feet per hour and may very well cover the connecting beach while you are out enjoying the spectacle of the East Quoddy Light and the ocean. If this should happen, you will be most unhappily trapped on the rocks without amenities for at least eight hours. Don't count on the Canadian Mounties or Coast Guard for rescue.

On your way back to the United States, notice the discontinued Mulholland Light. It stands just across the narrows from Lubec and can be seen on your right as you drive back over the international bridge toward U.S. soil.

WEST QUODDY HEAD LIGHT
West Quoddy Head, Maine - 1808

The name of this light is ironic since the tower stands on the easternmost point of land in the United States. Situated on a forty-foot-high cliff, the light overlooks Quoddy Narrows, which separates the United States from Canada. Across this channel lies Campobello Island with East Quoddy Head at its northeastern end; hence the name West Quoddy Head for the American light.

West Quoddy is among the oldest lights in Maine. Throughout the early years of the nineteenth century, citizens, merchants, and mariners operating out of the port of Passamaquoddy had demanded that a lighthouse be placed on West Quoddy Head. "We . . . take the liberty to suggest that the site [West Quoddy] on the mainland bank being forty feet above the water is the most projecting . . . and judicious that can be pitched upon for that purpose," they told their government.

By 1806 President Thomas Jefferson was convinced of the need and signed an order for construction of a lighthouse. By the end of the summer of 1808 all was in readiness, and keeper Thomas Dexter lit the first wicks in the lantern some ninety feet above sea level. According to early charts and guides, the light could be seen in clear weather from a distance of seven leagues (about three miles) at sea.

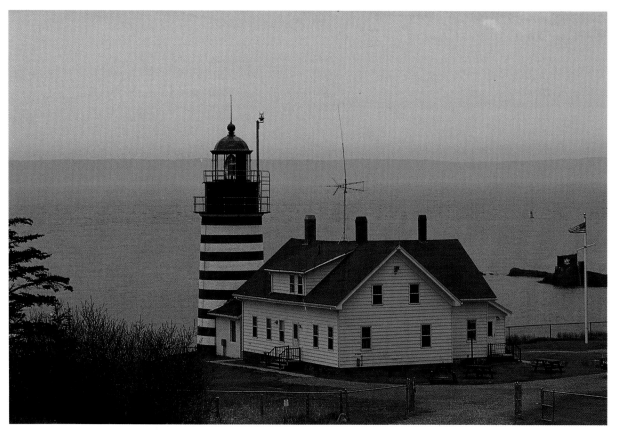

Red stripes distinguish West Quoddy Head Lighthouse, which, despite its name, stands on the easternmost point in the United States. The weather here is often violent. Patches of Arctic tundra grow within a few yards of the tower.

Dexter's pay was set at an unprincely $250 per year. Being a family man, Dexter soon discovered that he could not live on this paltry salary. He complained to his employers at the U.S. Treasury Department that the soil at West Quoddy was too poor for gardening and that he had to travel a considerable distance to purchase supplies. Dexter's government bosses must have had families themselves; mindful of his plight, they increased his salary—to $300 per year.

Among the chief worries of shipmasters passing near West Quoddy Head and its knife-edged Sail Rocks were the thick banks of fog that frequently billowed up out of the nearby Bay of Fundy. More than one ship got lost in the fog and came to grief on the rocks. To warn ships of the danger, a 500-pound bell was installed at the light station in 1820. During foggy weather, the keeper rang the bell at regular intervals, for which service he was paid an additional $70 per year. Unfortunately, mariners often could not hear the bell until they were far too close to the treacherous rocks. The station experimented with a high-pitched 241-pound bell, a deeper-throated 1,500-pounder, and finally, a huge triangular steel bar some fourteen feet in length. But none of the bells proved satisfactory.

In 1837 lighthouse inspector Captain Joseph Smith sailed past West Quoddy Head on the Revenue Cutter *Morris,* and it seems that he himself got lost in the fog. Smith later wrote a report that said the station needed "a sharp-toned bell of some 4,000 pounds weight." Apparently, Smith did not trust lighthouse keepers because he called for the bell to be "struck by machinery." Today, West Quoddy Head has a powerful foghorn activated by a robotic fog-sensing device.

On orders from the Lighthouse Board, the tower was pulled down and completely reconstructed in 1858. The new tower rises eighty-five feet above the sea, and for better daytime visibility, was painted with showy red-and-white stripes. This tower still stands today, its third-order Fresnel lens displaying a pair of two-second flashes four times each minute.

From U.S. 1 turn toward Lubec on Route 189. After approximately ten miles, turn right onto the road to Quoddy Head State Park and follow it for five miles to the lighthouse parking area. This is as far east as you can drive in the continental United States.

The lighthouse grounds are open to the public, but the tower and outbuildings are not. Both the lighthouse grounds and Quoddy Head State Park are closed at night and in winter.

The view here is spectacular. Cliffs drop down forty feet or more onto a stony beach, while a hundred yards or so offshore, waves crash over the Sail Rocks, which have torn through the hulls of many wooden sailing vessels. On the ocean horizon to the south lies Canada's enormous Grand Manan Island.

Take time to enjoy the State Park nature trails, which feature patches of true arctic tundra more often seen thousands of miles to the north. Among the cobblestones on the beach you occasionally find bricks that have been worn and rounded by the surf. These may be left over from the old 1808 lighthouse, which was demolished in 1858.

On the drive back toward Route 189 you can see the Lubec Channel Light rising out of the water on your right. Built in 1890, this white conical tower stands on a black cylindrical pier and is completely surrounded by the waters of the Lubec Channel. Because of their unusual shape, lighthouses of this type are often called "spark-plug lights."

PROSPECT HARBOR POINT LIGHT
Prospect Harbor, Maine - 1850

For more than a century fishermen have put to sea nearly every morning from Prospect Harbor. This small village remains one of the last strongholds of an old-time way of life that is under siege or has been entirely displaced elsewhere. As is the case in communities all along the coast of Maine, the sturdy Cape Cod cottages and captain's houses of Prospect Harbor are being bought up by frenzied real estate speculators and summer visitors, most of them from out of state. This has driven up prices and taxes, pushing many native villagers out of their homes. But lobster and sardine fishermen still live here, and each evening they are guided back home from the sea by the Prospect Harbor Point Light.

The light serves as a harbor marker and also warns boaters and fishermen away from the sharp, rocky protrusion of Prospect Point. The lantern displays a red light with two white flashes every six seconds. The light was left unstaffed after its last keeper, Captain Albion Faulkinham, retired in 1934.

Prospect Harbor had long been recognized as one of Maine's best anchorages when a lighthouse was finally placed here in 1850. The station was completely rebuilt and updated in 1891 on orders of the Lighthouse Board, but it has changed little in appearance since that time. Located on the east side of the inner harbor, the station consists of a small white conical tower and a detached keeper's cottage. Today, the station is part of a military base. The keeper's cottage is used as a guest house for the base.

Prospect Harbor Light guides lobster and sardine fishermen safely back to port each evening. The station is now part of a military base, and astronauts have rested from their adventures in the adjacent keeper's dwelling.

Prospect Harbor Point Lighthouse guides fishermen into and out of one of Maine's most scenic ports.

The drive to this light, which is only about an hour to the east of Acadia National Park, carries you into the heart of coastal Down East Maine. From U.S. 1 turn south on Route 195 or Route 186. A few miles' drive through gorgeous country on either road will bring you to Prospect Harbor village. A side road near the intersection of routes 186 and 195 will take you within a few hundred feet of the lighthouse. Since the light station is located on an active military base, it is closed to the public. But for an excellent view of the light and welcome stretch of your legs, you can park beside the road and walk out onto the red rocks leading down to the sea.

EGG ROCK LIGHT
Frenchman Bay, Maine - 1875

Located on a massive gray ledge at the entrance of Frenchman Bay, this light marks the seaward approaches to Bar Harbor, gateway to Acadia National Park. The ledge itself is utterly barren. Since the last lighthouse keeper left in 1966, it has been inhabited only by seals and seabirds. Many birds choose to make their nests on the isolated ledge. Perhaps that is how Egg Rock got its name.

Built in 1875 on orders of President Ulysses S. Grant, the station consists of a stubby tower perched atop a square keeper's house. This squat structure is certainly not among the more attractive lighthouses in New England. The Coast Guard further marred its looks by removing the lantern room and replacing the old prism lens with an airport-type beacon. Purists were not above referring to Egg Rock Light as the "ugliest lighthouse in Maine." Recently the Coast Guard reinstalled the lantern and restored the light to its original appearance.

Its looks do nothing to diminish its effectiveness, however, or the romance associated with it, as with all lighthouses. Millions of visitors to Acadia Park have seen and enjoyed its red, flashing light reaching out across Frenchman Bay. Egg Rock Light has been described as a "pillar of fire in the Atlantic."

Cruise-ship captains are always glad to see the light; so long as they have it in view, the dangers of Egg Rock ledge can easily be avoided. Inbound pleasure boaters are also happy to see the light. Once they sight it, they know that not far ahead lies a delightful anchorage at Bar Harbor and a boiled-lobster dinner.

Take Route 3 from Ellsworth to Acadia National Park. The light can probably best be viewed from one of the scenic overlooks on the road through the eastern side of the park. But a particularly spectacular view of Egg Rock Light and of other lighthouses in the area can be had from the summit of 1,530-foot Cadillac Mountain. The parking lot at the top of the mountain is closed after dark, but you can usually stay to see the light come on at Egg Rock.

You should plan to remain in the area long enough to enjoy the natural scenic wonders of Acadia as well as the shops and restaurants in Bar Harbor. Also, don't miss the elegant afternoon tea served each day at the Jordan Pond House inside the park. A longtime favorite of park visitors, the tea features hot popovers and jam and can be enjoyed at outdoor tables overlooking Jordan Pond.

Perched on a barren outcropping, Egg Rock Lighthouse guards the seaward approaches to Bar Harbor and Acadia National Park. The last keeper left in 1966 when the light was automated, and the rock is now inhabited only by seals and birds.

BAKER ISLAND LIGHT
Baker Island, Maine - 1828

Towering 105 feet above the lobster-rich waters at the southeastern edge of Frenchman Bay, this light crowns a pristine coastal island. Most of Baker Island's 123 acres are covered by a dense forest. Its rocky shores are visited regularly by seals and seabirds. The island is now part of Acadia National Park and, offering wondrous views of the mountains on nearby Mount Desert Island, is a favorite picnic spot for boaters.

Flashing once every ten seconds, Baker Island Light warns mariners of dangerous shoals and of a giant sandbar stretching from Baker Island to Little Cranberry Island to the northwest. The nation's sixth president, John Quincy Adams, ordered the lighthouse built in 1828. The Lighthouse Board had it rebuilt in 1855, placing a fourth-order Fresnel lens in the new tower. Looked after by keepers for more than 138 years, the light atop the stone tower has been automated since 1966. It is one of the nation's few solar-powered lighthouses.

An experimental, solar-powered station, Baker Island Lighthouse gathers energy from the sun during the day and uses it to guide mariners at night. The lighthouse stood at the center of a nineteenth-century legal squabble between the U.S. Government and the family of William Gilley, who was fired as keeper after twenty-one years of service.

The light's first keeper was William Gilley, who had once owned much of the island and had lived there for a long time. For reasons that were never made clear, the government fired Gilley after twenty-one years of service. The dismissal angered the old keeper's sons, Joseph and Elisha Gilley, who constantly hectored and harassed his replacement. The new keeper found it difficult even to land his boat on the island without a painful encounter with the Gilleys. Eventually, lighthouse officials went to court to have the Gilleys declared squatters and forcibly removed from Baker Island. The Gilleys, however, fired back with a countersuit, claiming that they, not the U.S. government, owned the island. The legal haggling was not resolved until late in the nineteenth century, when the Gilley heirs gained control of the entire island except for a small plot where the lighthouse and its outbuildings stood.

The lighthouse cannot be reached by land, but motorists can catch a glimpse of the light from the Acadia National Park perimeter road or from the summit of Cadillac Mountain. Boaters and day visitors to Baker Island can get a better, close-up view. The tower and grounds of the light are closed to the public. For more information, check with park headquarters at (207) 288–3338.

The old Fresnel lens that served here for almost a century was removed when the light was automated in 1966. It can now be seen in the Fisherman's Museum at Pemaquid Light in southern Maine.

BASS HARBOR HEAD LIGHT
Mount Desert Island, Maine – 1858

Among the most picturesque lighthouses anywhere, Bass Harbor Head Light is seen and photographed each year by countless thousands of visitors to Acadia National Park. Clinging to a rocky promontory, the structure consists of a small white tower attached to a modest dwelling.

Established by the Lighthouse Board in 1858, during the presidency of James Buchanan, the light marked the entrance to Blue Hill Bay on the west side of Mount Desert Island. It also assisted vessels moving in and out of Bass Harbor. The lighthouse continues to provide these same services to mariners today. Fishermen and pleasure boaters keep an eye out for its red light, which occults briefly every four seconds. (Occulting lights show longer periods of light than of darkness. Early occulting lights were often mechanically eclipsed so that they appeared to blink on and off.)

Rocks in the vicinity of Bass Harbor Head show signs of scouring by ice. The same glacial forces that transformed the Maine coast into a maze of inlets and promontories also carved deep channels into stony Mount Desert Island. Not far to the north of the lighthouse is a geological wonder seen nowhere else in America—a fjord. Much like the well-known fjords of Norway, Mount Desert's Somes Sound is long, narrow, and walled in by steep cliffs. Sculpted from solid rock by a glacier, the sound is a testament to the power of moving ice.

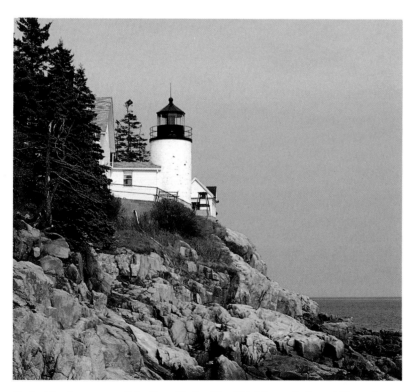

Bathed in afternoon sunlight, Bass Harbor Head Lighthouse is framed like a picture on a postcard.

From Ellsworth, drive toward Acadia National Park on Route 3. Shortly after crossing over to Mount Desert Island, turn right on Route 198. Turn right again on Route 102 at Somesville, where you can get a look at Somes Sound, America's only true fjord. Drive past Echo Lake and through the village of Southwest Harbor, a wonderful place for shopping and dining. Just beyond Bass Harbor, a dirt road leads to the lighthouse parking lot. For more information, contact Acadia National Park at (207) 288–3338.

For lobster lovers: The best meals are not always had at fancy restaurants. Several roadside stands in this area offer boiled lobster and corn on the cob at bargain prices.

GREAT DUCK ISLAND LIGHT
South of Bass Harbor, Maine - 1890

Great Duck Island lies in the open Atlantic more than 5 miles to the southeast of Bass Harbor. The lighthouse was recently automated, but for nearly a century it was staffed by up to four keepers, who usually housed their families on the island with them. These families lived for weeks and even months at a stretch with little or no contact with the mainland. They could see the mountains of Mount Desert Island on the horizon to the north, but otherwise, their world was an island about one and a half miles in circumference, covered by a stunted forest opening here and there onto grassy meadows.

Still, the keepers made the best of their tiny world. They hunted, fished, told stories, and even maintained a school for their children. At certain times the Great Duck Island school could boast a larger student population than some of the smaller one- or two-room schoolhouses on the mainland. One keeper had sixteen children on the island with him.

Rough weather often prevented the delivery of mail for weeks at a time. When the wind stopped howling, the ocean calmed, and the mail boat could put to sea to make its deliveries, the Great Duck keepers would receive several bushel baskets of letters, magazines, and outdated newspapers.

The keepers finally got telephone service during World War II, but the cable, laid at considerable expense across the sea floor from Mount Desert Island, was not intended for the convenience of the families on the island. The military hoped the keepers would provide early warning of German submarines prowling the coast. Fearing attack from the sea, some keepers moved their families off the island during the war, but no such attack ever came.

The only invasion of Great Duck Island was the one mounted regularly by hunters armed with shotguns and birding rifles. The island takes its name from a large freshwater pond near its center where, it is said, thousands of ducks and other waterfowl once nested. In time, mainland hunters killed off or drove away these enormous flocks.

The island has seen its share of human death and tragedy as well, much of it the result of cruel weather and shipwreck. Keepers used to tell the story of a horrible wreck during a harsh winter gale. An entire crew was lost when their ship slammed into the rocks on the northeast side of the island. The keepers found only two bodies, a pair of sailors locked together in a grizzly, frozen embrace. Since travel to the mainland was impossible, the two were buried in a common grave on the island. The ground was frozen so hard that the keepers had to use picks to dig the grave. For many years keepers maintained a tradition of laying a wreath each Memorial Day on the grave of the frozen sailors.

Flashing once every ten seconds, the red Great Duck Island Light helps mariners avoid most such encounters with the island's deadly rocks.

Neither the forty-two-foot tower nor its red light, flashing from sixty-seven feet above the sea, can be seen easily from land. They are best viewed from the air or from a boat passing on the south side of the island.

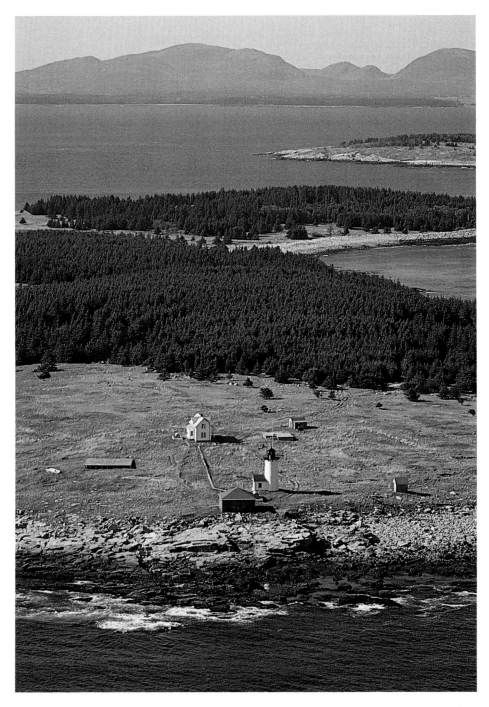

Named for the mighty flocks of waterfowl that gathered here until hunters decimated them, Great Duck Island is a lonely outpost. No one lives here now, but the island once had a thriving school for the children of lighthouse keepers. The Nature Conservancy maintains a wildlife preserve on the island.

MOUNT DESERT ROCK LIGHT
Mount Desert Rock, Maine - 1830

On a rare calm December day shortly before Christmas in 1977, a helicopter settled onto the landing pad at Mount Desert Rock some twenty-six miles out in the Atlantic Ocean. A pair of eager young Coast Guardsmen, Robin Runnels, twenty-two, of Hyannis, Massachusetts, and Douglas Nute, twenty, of St. Louis, Missouri, tossed their gear into the chopper, hopped aboard, and strapped themselves in. They were more than ready to go. As the chopper lifted off and sped them on their way toward a welcome holiday with their families, the pair took full advantage of a gull's-eye view of the light station that would never again be their home. After the holidays, they would take on new assignments somewhere far from the isolation of Mount Desert Rock. And the old lighthouse, its light and foghorn now fully automated, would continue to do its job—alone.

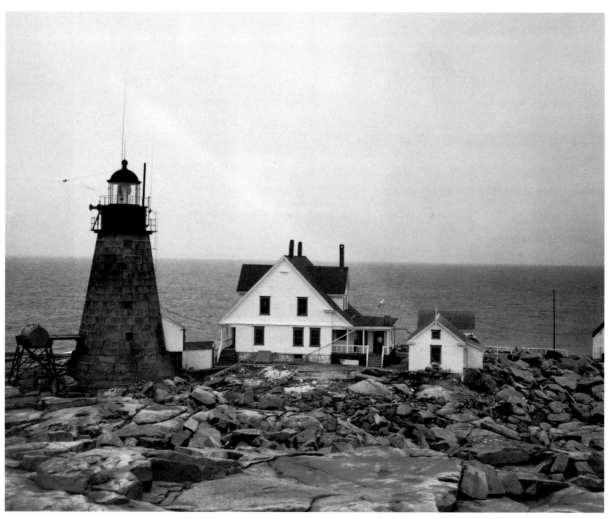

Located twenty-six miles out in the Atlantic, Mount Desert Rock ranks among the nation's most isolated light stations. Before the light was automated in 1977, the station served for almost 150 years as a lonely home to keepers and their families. (Courtesy U.S. Coast Guard)

Runnels and Nute are the last names on a long list of keepers who have served time on "the rock," surely among the loneliest of the Coast Guard light stations. If the Great Duck Island keepers thought they were isolated, those on Mount Desert Rock must have thought they were serving on the moon. An exceptionally dangerous obstacle for shipping, Mount Desert Rock is, indeed, little more than a rock. An open ocean ledge, it measures only 600 yards by 200 yards, and its highest point stands only twenty feet above the play of the sea.

Hardly anything grows naturally on the rock. Traditionally, lobstermen and other friends of the keepers brought baskets of soil to the station each spring. The keepers spread the dirt near the lighthouse or stuffed it into rain-moistened cracks and crevasses so that they would have a place to plant a garden and grow a few flowers. Usually, before the growing season was over, a stormy sea would rise up and wash away the blooms, the vegetables, and the soil, leaving behind only the bare rock.

The first lighthouse erected here in 1830 was a two-story cottage with a lantern set on its roof. This arrangement placed the light fifty-six feet above mean sea level, not high enough to serve the heavy shipping traffic in these waters properly. When the Lighthouse Board was formed by act of Congress in 1851, one of its first actions was to authorize $10,000 for renovation of the light station at Mount Desert Rock. Because of the station's remote location, the work took several years to complete, but by 1857 a stone tower had raised the light slightly, to a height of sixty feet. Even with a powerful third-order Fresnel lens installed in the lantern, however, the light was still thought to be inadequate. Some decades later, in 1893, the tower was rebuilt again, this time raising the light to seventy-five feet above the sea. The new granite tower had a broad base and walls as thick as those of a fortress to help it withstand angry seas.

Although the light was effective, it could not prevent the ocean tug *Astral* from slamming into Mount Desert Rock shortly before dawn on December 9, 1902. Despite sub-zero temperatures, the station's keepers managed to save all but one member of the tug's "more or less frozen" eighteen-man crew. (Please see page 6 for a description of the incident.)

While neither the lighthouse nor the ledge it stands on can be seen from land, the light, flashing white at fifteen-second intervals, is a welcome sight for boaters and sailors in the area. The lighthouse also can be seen from the air. Small planes can be chartered at Bar Harbor Airport on Route 3.

BURNT COAT HARBOR
(HOCKAMOCK HEAD) LIGHT
Swans Island, Maine - 1872

Why the name Burnt Coat? During the early seventeenth century, a great fire consumed much of the dense forest and other growth on what is today known as Swans Island. A party of French sailors who briefly visited the charred and inhospitable island supposedly gave it the name *Brun Côte* or "Brown Coast." Since the French words twisted the tongues of later English-speaking settlers, the name became Burnt Coat. Or so it is said.

Another, equally plausible, explanation for the name may lie with the island's first permanent resident, Thomas Kench. Driven half mad by the violence of the American Revolution, Kench deserted the Continental Army in 1776 and escaped to this remote place, where he lived as a hermit, far from the drums and destruction of war. As a deserter, he was said to have "burned his coat" or uniform; hence the name.

A squatter, Kench lived alone on the nine-square-mile island for more than a decade, but his peace and solitude could not last forever. Imagine Kench's dismay when his former commanding officer, Colonel James Swan, showed up and bought the island out from under him. One of the original Sons of Liberty, Swan had participated in the Boston Tea Party in 1773 and fought hard against the British during the Revolutionary War. But having helped rid the country of a king, Swan quickly grew tired of democracy and decided to carve out a kingdom of his own in the coastal north. Swan's royal aspirations proved financially ruinous, however, and he ended his days in a debtors' prison in Paris.

But Swans Island crowned another "king" with the arrival of David Smith. A strong-willed man, known to friend and foe alike as "King David," Smith took it upon himself single-handedly to populate the island. He eventually fathered twenty-four children, who further increased his tribe with more than fifty grandchildren. Smith's descendants have lived on the island for two centuries and have watched vessel after vessel pile up on the ship-killing ledges near Burnt Coat Harbor.

Burnt Coat appears a tempting refuge to a sea captain caught in a storm, but all too often, a ship making a run for the harbor ends up on the rocks. In 1872 the Lighthouse Board tried to help by building a pair of towers intended to serve as "range lights." As with range lights elsewhere, the towers were built some distance apart, with the rear lantern at a greater elevation. Mariners who saw the lights lined up one atop the other knew they were in a safe channel. Unfortunately, this arrangement tended to confuse local sailors, and wrecks occurred at an even faster pace than before. So, in 1885 the Board decided to simplify matters by pulling down the smaller of the two lighthouses. The second lighthouse, on Hockamock Head at the mouth of the harbor, still stands. Perched on a square tower forty-seven feet above the water, the lantern displays a green light occulting briefly every four seconds.

Despite the presence of the light, ships continued over the years to slam into the Swans Island rocks. As a result, the islanders have made an industry out of emptying the hulls of wrecked vessels. They have salvaged lumber, coal, and all sorts of other freight. Of course, they have found some cargoes more useful than others. On January 27, 1888, a certain Captain Brett at the helm of a fine schooner tried to duck out of a squall into the calm water of Burnt Coat Harbor. Unable to see in the thick weather, he missed the harbor altogether and ran up onto the stony shore. Brett and all six members of his crew escaped the disaster without injury—but not so the people of Swans Island. Following the storm, they gathered at the site of the wreck expecting to benefit from the salvage of a large cargo. They discovered, however, that the schooner holds were loaded to the hatches with turnips. No doubt the dogged salvagers ate turnips every day until nobody on the island could ever again stand the sight of the things.

Although situated several miles from the mainland, Swans Island can be reached via a car ferry operating daily out of Bass Harbor on Mount Desert Island. The ferry makes six round trips each day during the summer and four each day during the off-season. For schedule information and reservations call the Maine Ferry Service at (207) 244–3254. Unless you are traveling in July and August, you should take food and drink with you. Very few businesses on Swans Island are open during the off-season.

A few miles north of Swans Island stands the Blue Hill Bay Lighthouse on a scrap of ground with the well-chosen name of Fly Island. The island is quite low, and most of it disappears at high tide. The squat tower is no taller than the attached one-and-a-half-story keeper's dwelling. The lantern displays a green light that flashes once every four seconds.

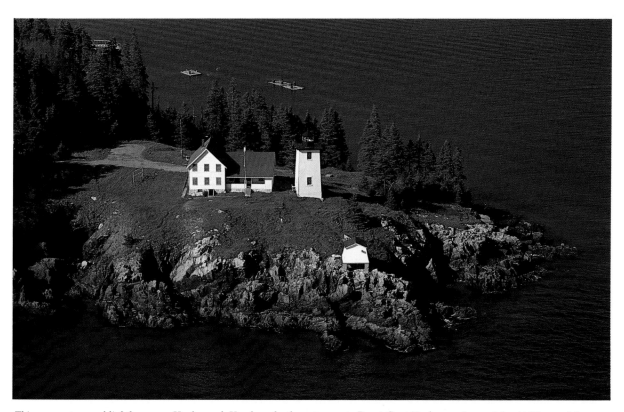

This square-towered lighthouse on Hockamock Head marks the entrance to Burnt Coat Harbor on Swans Island. Weary of democracy, former patriot and Revolutionary War soldier James Swan tried, but failed, to carve out a kingdom for himself on this island during the late 1700s.

SADDLEBACK LEDGE LIGHT
Isle au Haut Bay, Maine - 1839

Saddleback Ledge is a bare scrap of rock exposed on all sides to the rush of the sea. A forty-two-foot, cone-shaped gray stone tower has stood on the ledge since 1839, its flashing white light warning sailors against collision with the rock and certain calamity. The light was automated in 1954, but until that time, it was continuously staffed. Perhaps no station in the Lighthouse Service ever placed its keepers more at the mercy of the elements.

Winter squalls swoop down on the ledge with such ferocity that their huge breakers are said to sweep completely over the rock and the lighthouse itself. But even in moderate seas, Saddleback could be a dangerous place for its keepers. Getting on or off the ledge was especially risky. W. W. Wells, a keeper whose colorful descriptions were legendary even among his salty comrades, describes how he almost lost his life while trying to land a small open boat at Saddleback:

"During the severe part of January 1925, while landing at the station, my boat was capsized, and had it not been for a lobster fisherman I would have gone to Davy Jones's locker. I had just come from a furlough and was trying to make a landing when a mountainous sea rushed in from the ocean, overturning my boat and sending me flying into the water. Why, it turned me upside down quicker than you could say "Jack Robinson." I was heavily dressed at the time with long hip boots, oil pants, overalls, three shirts, and a heavy sweater. I had no chance to swim with that outfit about my body and legs. . . . I was just about ready to give up when George Wells [no relation], a lobster fisherman, came along in his thirty-foot powerboat and hauled me out of the water. If I ever wanted to be reconciled with my Maker, I did right then. I just simply thought that my day of reckoning had come."

The light, flashing once every six seconds, can be seen from nearby islands, but the lighthouse itself is all but inaccessible. Landing a boat on the ledge is difficult and very dangerous. The lighthouse can be seen from the air or from a boat.

The tower of Saddleback Ledge Lighthouse still clings to its exposed rock, all traces of dwellings and outbuildings swept away by wind, water, and time.

ISLE AU HAUT LIGHT
Isle au Haut, Maine - 1907

A gleaming white cylinder set on a tall base of rough-cut granite, this lighthouse is as lovely as it is unique. The same might be said of the pristine island on which the lighthouse stands. Its densely forested hills soar hundreds of feet above the Atlantic, and along with the mountains of Mount Desert Island, are often the first land spotted by mariners sailing northwestward out of the Atlantic. In 1604 the French explorer Samuel de Champlain saw these heights rising blue above the ocean horizon, and landing on the island, found it delightful. Later, in a book about his explorations and adventures, Champlain described the place as "high and striking" and gave it the name *Isle Haute* or "high island." Today it is known as Isle au Haut.

The people of Isle au Haut have always been an enterprising breed. During the early 1800s they fished, raised sheep, and operated a thriving saltworks. Meanwhile, sea captains from Isle au Haut sailed halfway around the world in their

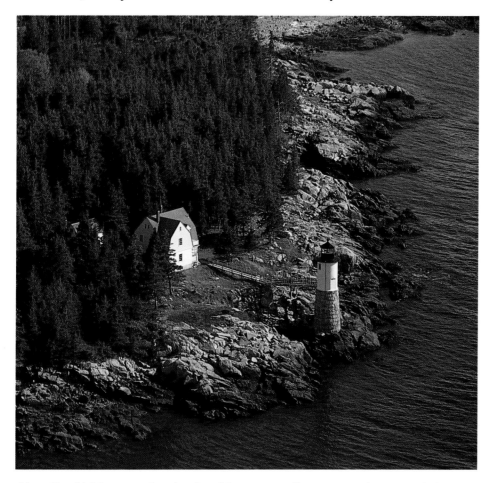

Isle au Haut Lighthouse stands at the edge of the water; a walkway connects the tower to the keeper's house, now a bed-and-breakfast inn.

fast clipper ships to trade with China. By 1860 watermen here were canning their own lobster meat and selling it to London's Crosse & Blackwell. Later they helped create a new dining tradition in New York City by sailing to Manhattan each week with a cargo of hundreds of live Maine lobsters.

Although the rich waters around Isle au Haut continue to yield bounteous catches of lobster, most island residents now make their living from the tourist trade. In recent decades, the year-round population has dropped to only a few dozen, but the island is crowded in July and August. As in communities throughout coastal Maine, many of the fine old homes on Isle au Haut are boarded up most of the year but are filled with light and laughter during the summer. An offshore extension of Acadia National Park, which takes up more than half of the island, attracts plenty of hikers and campers from the mainland.

But even in the summer, Isle au Haut remains a quiet retreat. The island has kept much of its rustic, old-time atmosphere. Most houses still have no electricity, so visitors must read their sea stories or *Down East* magazines by gaslight. It was only a few years ago that residents finally gave up on their antique, "Grandma Bell" telephone system—with the last operating crank-style telephones in the nation.

The lighthouse stands on the rocks just off Robinson's Point, its granite base washed twice each day by the high tide. A simple white bridge connects the forty-eight-foot tower to the mainland and the keeper's house, which now serves as a bed-and-breakfast inn. Among the few Maine lighthouses built in this century, the light guides fishermen and pleasure boaters passing by Isle au Haut. The beacon flashes red every four seconds.

The island is served year-round by a ferry operating out of Stonington on Deer Island. To reach Stonington, turn off U.S. 1 near the village of Orland and follow Route 15 for approximately forty miles. Route 15 will carry you through some of the earth's most lovely countryside and through Blue Hill, one of Maine's most attractive country towns. The Blue Hill Fair, held each year in September, was the model for the fair in Charlotte's Web, E. B. White's well-known children's novel. From Blue Hill, a brief side trip on routes 172 and 175 will bring you to Blue Hill Falls, a tumbling rapid that reverses direction with the tides. A working fishing village, Stonington itself is worth the drive. Ferry hours vary with the season. For schedules and reservations call (207) 367-2468.

EAGLE ISLAND LIGHT
Eagle Island, Maine - 1839

For more than a century an enormous fog bell stood beside the Eagle Island Lighthouse at the top of a sheer, 100-foot cliff overlooking the eastern passage through Penobscot Bay. In fog and heavy weather the keeper struck the 1,200-pound brass bell at regular intervals to warn the masters of ships plowing blindly through the passage that dangerous rocks lay nearby. Then the Coast Guard decided to automate and unman the lighthouse. Since there was no longer a keeper to sound the bell, its duties were taken over by buoys out in the channel.

During the summer of 1964 the Coast Guard sent a cutter to the island with a crew of muscular Mainers to remove the big, out-of-work bell. But the massive bell proved more than a match for the burly laborers trying to wrestle it down the hill to the cutter. Something went wrong, and men started shouting. Fortunately for the workers, they all managed to get out of the way as the bell began to roll down toward the cliff. Over it went, banging, clanging, and ringing out like the gongs of hell. When the bell hit the sea, it sent a geyser of water skyward. Then, as the echoes of the bell's clamor died away, members of the crew up on the cliff eyed

Eagle Island Lighthouse gleams in stark contrast to the dark green of surrounding trees.

one another sheepishly and shrugged their shoulders. It is easy to imagine one of them saying: "Well, fellas, we got that rascal down the hill in a wicked hurry and that's for sure."

The Coast Guard workers figured they would leave well enough alone, and for several months, the bell lay in the ocean, part of it exposed at each low tide. One day, while working his pots below the Eagle Island cliffs, an enterprising lobsterman named Walter Shepard spotted the bell and got an idea. Shepard hooked a heavy chain to the fallen fog bell and painstakingly towed it several miles through the ocean. Today, the salvaged bell is located on Great Spruce Head outside the family home of noted nature photographer Eliot Porter. There it continues to ring out, serving the Porter family as, perhaps, the world's most impressive dinner bell.

First lit in 1839, during the administration of the nation's eighth president, Martin Van Buren, the Eagle Island Light guides ships over Hardhead Shoals and into the Penobscot Bay. One of a chain of lights including those at Dice Head and Fort Point near the mouth of the Penobscot River, it helped mark a clear path through the rocky bay for a host of nineteenth-century lumber ships. The need for such a well-marked route was clear, since mills were shipping prodigious amounts of lumber down to the sea from Maine's heartland forests. During the mid-1880s, shippers loaded more than eight billion board feet of lumber at the inland port of Bangor.

Standing a lofty 106 feet above the water, the light's whitewashed conical tower lifts its lantern just above the treetops on the northeast end of the island. Having changed little since a major renovation in 1858, it continues to guide mariners with its white light, flashing once every four seconds.

The Eagle Island Light can only be reached by water, but to pass this lighthouse by boat can be an extraordinary experience. Sailors headed either north or south through the channel between Eagle and Deer islands will see the white tower rise up suddenly, a ghostly giant standing on a forested cliff. Eagle Island is itself a gem, rich in trees, cranberries, and history. To avoid confusion, please keep in mind that Maine has several Eagle Islands. The one in Casco Bay, roughly 100 miles to the southwest, was the home of Admiral Robert E. Peary, the first man to reach the North Pole.

DICE HEAD LIGHT
Castine, Maine - 1829

Among the oldest and most romantic towns anywhere in America is Castine, a cluster of old summer cottages and even older sea captain's houses arrayed on a blunt arrow of land pointing directly into Penobscot Bay. Since it guards the entrance to the Penobscot River, seafarers have always coveted this strategic peninsula. As a result, the flags of at least four nations have fluttered above its forts, and the smoke of musket and cannon fire has drifted out across the river many times.

A band of French fur traders established a settlement here in 1614. They were displaced by rival traders from the Plymouth Bay Colony in 1629. The French

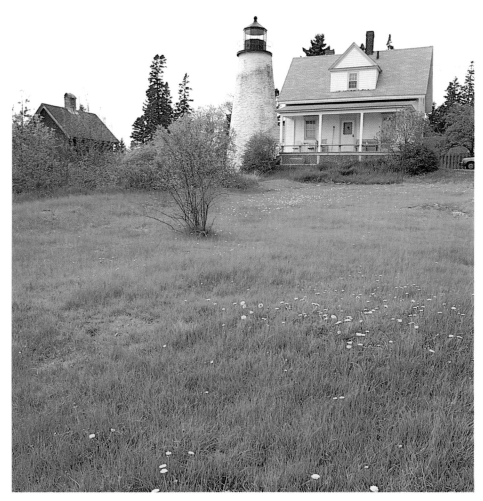

Shown here under siege by dandelions, the old Dice Head Lighthouse has been dark for many years. The people of Castine, one of New England's oldest and most storied villages, maintain the lighthouse and keeper's dwelling, which commands a world-class view of Penobscot Bay.

returned in 1635, but the British Navy drove them out again in 1654. It seemed that nobody could hold the area for long. Dutch pirates overran the town's garrison in 1674. Then came the Baron de St. Castine, a wealthy French adventurer who brought peace to the town by marrying the daughter of a troublesome Indian chief named Madockawanda.

By the time the Revolutionary War broke out, the British flag once again flew over the peninsula. In 1779 Paul Revere arrived with an army of Americans who scaled the cliffs along the Penobscot Bay and stormed Fort George at the top of the hill above the town. The first assault failed, and Revere's troops never got a chance to regroup and try another. A small British squadron surprised and scattered their supply fleet, sinking nearly forty vessels.

At the start of the War of 1812, the Americans had a fort of their own at Castine, this one named for a president rather than a king. But the defenders of Fort Madison were no match for the huge British fleet that swept down on them early in the war. They fired off a few desultory shots in the general direction of the British ships, spiked their guns, and fled inland as fast as their legs could take them. The British held the town for the balance of the war, billeting their officers and men in private homes and other buildings, many of which still stand.

In 1829 the Lighthouse Service built a tower on Dice Head to help guide lumber ships and other vessels in and out of the Penobscot River. The lighthouse also served to call home the clipper ships of Castine captains on the last leg of trading adventures that often took them as far away as China. Today, Castine's harbor is filled with pleasure craft during the summer months, though the clipper ships are gone, along with the crusty sea dogs who sailed them. But young men and women still go down to the sea from Castine. Near the earthen walls of old Fort George is the campus of the Maine Maritime Academy, which offers first-rate degree programs for aspiring merchant seamen.

The Lighthouse Board rebuilt the Dice Head tower in 1858, giving it a six-sided shape and attaching to it an excellent keeper's dwelling. Both the tower and the dwelling are still in good repair, but the lantern has been dark for decades. Its job was long ago taken over by an automated light perched atop a simple skeleton structure down on the rocks beside the bay. The light flashes white every four seconds and can be seen for approximately ten miles.

From U.S. 1 take Route 175 south and then Route 166 or 166A to Castine. Keep your camera handy. This is an outstanding scenic drive, and you may catch a glimpse of the Fort Point Lighthouse across the bay in Searsport. In Castine, follow Battle Avenue to the lighthouse, which stands on the crest of Dice Head. A public path and wooden stairway lead down to the bay, where a small modern daymark and navigational light is located. While you are gawking at the scenery, a seal may pop its head out of the water to have a look at you.

Be sure to leave time for a tour of this fine old town. Much of the architecture is nineteenth-century, and wooden markers tell the stories of the many battles fought here. If visiting during the summer, consider having dinner at the Castine Inn, a delightfully unpretentious Down East hostelry. You will want more biscuits. You may also want to buy a copy of the Castine Patriot, a straight-talking, small-town New England newspaper. The author was once its editor.

FORT POINT LIGHT
Searsport, Maine - 1836

During the mid-nineteenth century, as many as 200 lumber ships might pass the square-towered Fort Point Light in a single week. All of them were on their way to or from the bustling inland port of Bangor, about twenty-five miles up the Penobscot River.

Built in 1836 by order of President Andrew Jackson, the lighthouse, along with the lights at Eagle Island and Dice Head, pointed the way into the mouth of the river and beyond to the world's busiest lumber port. Over the years, billions of board feet of lumber, cut from Maine's tall forests, moved down the river past the light. The wood was used to build homes, businesses, bridges, and fences in Boston and other cities along the East Coast.

Although not much taller than the attached keeper's dwelling, the tower stands on a high promontory, its light eighty-eight feet above the water. The lantern still contains the same Fresnel prism lens installed when the Lighthouse Board decided to renovate the station in 1857. It displays a fixed white light. The fogbell house still stands and is one of the last of its kind.

Near the lighthouse are the ruins of Fort Pownall, a key military outpost established in 1759 during the French and Indian War. The British and American armies fought two battles here during the Revolutionary War.

Turn off U.S. 1 toward Penobscot Bay at Stockton Springs and follow signs to Fort Point State Park and the Fort Pownall Memorial. Occupied by a state park employee, the keeper's dwelling is closed to the public. The lighthouse grounds offer a sweeping view of the bay.

Fort Point Lighthouse is reflected in a window of the building housing the station fog bell. The building is listed in the National Register of Historic Places; the fog bell is a rare survivor of the old lighthouse establishment.

MATINICUS ROCK LIGHT
South of Matinicus Island, Maine - 1827

Located about twenty five miles from Rockland, the nearest mainland port, Matinicus Rock is truly a remote outpost. Fog blankets the treeless island one out of every five days. When there is no fog, wind tears at the rock, and storms blast it with such fury that giant boulders are shifted by the surf. Exposed to the very worst the sea can throw at it, this would seem an unlikely place to build a lighthouse with wood. But that is exactly what the Lighthouse Service did, throwing up two relatively flimsy wooden towers on the island in 1827.

John Shaw, the station's first keeper, must have shaken his head in dismay at the sight of the white, wood-frame towers. They would surely fall in the first muscular nor'easter. But, surprisingly, the towers stood up to the sea's anger a lot longer than did Shaw. Already sixty-five years old when he took over the new station, Shaw fell desperately ill during his third year as keeper. By early the next year, the old man was dead, the life drummed out of him by the sea and the rock.

Although most of them were much younger than Shaw, few of the keepers who followed him lasted very long on the rock. During its first decade, the station killed or drove off its keepers at an average of one every two years.

The wooden towers themselves endured for just under twenty years, but by 1846 they were totally ramshackle and had to be replaced. This time the builders used granite. Ironically, the new stone towers lasted only half as long as the wooden towers before them. In 1857 the Lighthouse Board pulled them down and erected the taller cut-granite towers that still stand on the island today. Only one of the towers remains in use, however. Its white light flashes once every ten seconds.

Surely the rock's most remarkable resident was its heroine, Abbie Burgess. She was only seventeen in 1856 when a stubborn gale blew up out of the Atlantic and cut the station off from the mainland for nearly four weeks. When the storm hit, keeper Samuel Burgess was in Rockland buying supplies for his family and medicine for his bedridden wife. He had left his daughter Abbie to look after his sick wife and three younger daughters. Also, having taught Abbie to trim the wicks of the fourteen lamps in each of the two towers, he counted on her to keep the all-important Matinicus Rock lights burning.

The storm struck suddenly, packing winds so strong that boats could make no headway against them. Trapped in Rockland, Burgess could do nothing to help his family. As days stretched into weeks, with no break in the relentless gale, the keeper despaired. But sea captains who had fought their way out of the storm into the safety of Rockland's calm harbor brought hope. Those who had passed close to Matinicus Rock said they had seen lights in the towers.

After nearly a month, the winds finally let up, and Burgess was able to sail back home. What he found there astonished him. The storm had destroyed much of the light station. Only the foundation of the keeper's dwelling remained; the rest had been washed into the sea. But thanks to Abbie, the Burgess family had survived. As the first dark clouds bore down on the rock, she had moved her mother and sisters out of the dwelling and into one of the stone towers. There she had

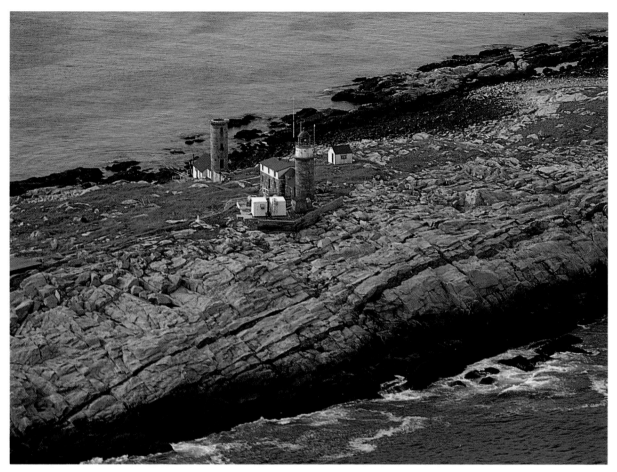

Located about 25 miles out in the Atlantic, Matinicus Rock Lighthouse was among the most isolated, challenging, and dangerous duty stations for keepers. Now automated, the station is home to a large colony of puffins.

cared for them and kept their spirits high, and never once in four weeks had she let the lights fail.

Eventually, Abbie married the son of a lighthouse keeper, and together, they kept the twin lights of Matinicus Rock. She had four children, all of them born on the rock. Abbie Burgess Grant is buried in the Forest Hills Cemetery on Spruce Head Island. Her gravestone is a replica of her lighthouse.

The classical Fresnel lens that once shined on Matinicus Rock is now on display at the Shore Village Museum in Rockland, Maine. This is one of the best and most complete lighthouse museums in the country. For information or directions to Abbie's grave, call (207) 594–0311.

Special arrangements can sometimes be made with local boating companies for trips to the island. Visits usually require an overnight stay on rustic Matinicus Island, about six miles north of the rock. For ferry information call (207) 366–3700. During the spring and summer months, a large colony of colorful puffins nests on the rock. Access to the island is restricted, especially during puffin mating season. The trip is well worth the time, since seven or eight lighthouses can be viewed from the boat, and finback whale sightings are not unusual.

A Fresnel lens concentrates light with hundreds of highly polished glass prisms. The government fitted most American lighthouses with Fresnels during the mid-1800s. This second-order lens at Boston Light has sent its flash seaward since 1859.

CHAPTER TWO

LIGHTS OF
THE WINTER COAST

Southern Coast of Maine

Lights of the Winter Coast

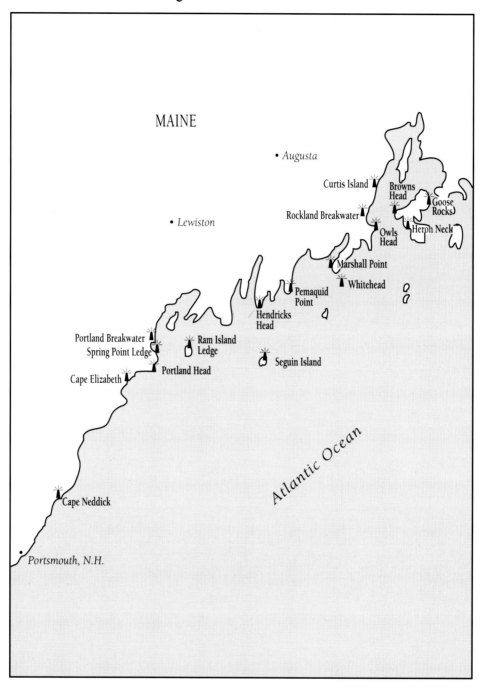

MAINE

• *Augusta*

• *Lewiston*

Curtis Island

Browns
Head

Goose
Rocks

Rockland Breakwater

Heron Neck

Owls
Head

Marshall Point

Whitehead

Pemaquid
Point

Hendricks
Head

Portland Breakwater

Ram Island
Ledge

Spring Point Ledge

Portland Head

Seguin Island

Cape Elizabeth

Atlantic Ocean

Cape Neddick

• *Portsmouth, N.H.*

In Maine waters mariners fear the cold more than the deep. This is especially true in winter, when a shipwrecked sailor is far more likely to freeze to death than to drown. Seamen and fishermen in these parts dread the gales that roll in from the northeast and the blizzards that sweep down out of Canada. These storms often cause temperatures to drop so low that the salt spray from the waves pounding on the side of the ship rattles onto the deck like hail. Ice grips everything, encrusting the hulls and masts of schooners, locking up the clappers of fog bells, and obscuring the windows of lighthouses. Not surprisingly, wrecks are more common in winter than at other times.

The stories of disaster and rescue told by Maine's lighthouse keepers often crackle with ice. They are the sort of tales that should only be told on a summer day or at least beside a warm fire with a hot mug to steady the hand. The following stories have been retold many times and have emptied countless pots of coffee.

THE GHOST SHIP *ISIDORE*

In a graveyard at Kennebunkport is a stone bearing the name of Captain Leander Foss. The body of Captain Foss, however, does not rest anywhere near the stone. It is assumed that Foss went to Davy Jones's locker along with his handsome bark, which disappeared under strange circumstances off Cape Neddick in 1842. But some say Foss still sails the seas as captain of the ghost ship *Isidore.*

A seaman named Thomas King was supposed to ship out with the *Isidore* when it set sail from Kennebunkport on the last day of November 1842. But two days before the scheduled departure, King woke up in a cold sweat from a terrible dream: a vision of a wrecked ship and drowning sailors. King had no doubt that the vessel in his nightmare was the bark *Isidore* and the dying men were his fellow crewmen.

King told Foss about his ominous dream, but the old sea captain laughed at him. When Foss refused to delay the *Isidore*'s sailing, King begged to be let out of his contract and left behind. At this point Captain Foss put on a stern face, reminded King that he had already received a month's salary in advance, and told the frightened seaman in the plainest of language to be aboard the *Isidore* when it pulled away from the dock.

The following night, another member of the *Isidore* crew had a disturbing dream. This sailor saw seven coffins and saw himself in one of them. Foss heard about this second nightmare, but having little respect for superstition and a schedule to keep, he made up his mind to sail first thing the next morning.

As November 30 dawned, the families and friends of the *Isidore*'s crew gathered at the Kennebunkport wharfs to wish their loved ones well. But a cloud of dread and gloom hung heavy over the farewell, and there was little of the usual cheering and hat waving as the bark glided slowly out of the harbor. By this time, the sky had added a few dark clouds of its own to the scene, and they quickly increased in size and number. It began to snow, and a bitter-cold wind came up out of the north to hurry the *Isidore* rapidly down toward the sea and into the realm of legend.

Among those who watched the *Isidore*'s masts disappear in the snowy distance was Thomas King. He hid in the woods until he was certain the bark was underway. King expected his acquaintances in town to scorch his ears for having jumped ship, and they did. But his disgrace lasted only about one day.

On the following morning, word came to Kennebunkport that pieces of a large ship were scattered all along the shore in the vicinity of Cape Neddick. It was the *Isidore*. There were no survivors of the wreck, and only seven bodies washed ashore, one of them the sailor who had dreamed about the seven coffins. The body of Captain Foss was never found.

Imaginative residents and visitors to Maine's scenic coast have reported many sightings of the *Isidore* during the century and a half since the wreck. They describe a close-reefed bark and shadowy figures who stand motionless on the deck and stare straight ahead. Maybe Thomas King later saw the phantom ship himself—in his dreams if not with his eyes. But if he ever again encountered the ghostly *Isidore,* he never said so.

THE FROZEN LOVERS

A few days before Christmas, in the year 1850, a small coasting schooner dropped anchor off Jameson's Point. The vessel was without its captain, who had gone ashore in nearby Rockland and mysteriously disappeared. Some say the captain had been fired; others say he had a premonition and decided to flee from fate. But the schooner's mate, who knew nothing of any dark premonition, saw his master's absence as an opportunity. He had recently proposed to a lovely young woman, and with no one to order him otherwise, he invited her to his cabin.

Only the mate, his bride-to-be, and a deckhand were aboard on the evening of December 22, when a vicious winter gale blew in off the ocean and snapped the schooner's cables. Although the sailors fought hard to save their vessel, the storm drove it relentlessly forward, finally crushing its hull on the cruel ledges near Owls Head. Held in a vice-like grip by the rocks, the schooner filled with sea water but did not sink. Instead, it became a target for giant waves, which threw spouts of freezing spray over the three frightened people huddled on its deck. Their clothes and even their skin quickly became rough and crusty with ice.

The mate knew that he and his fellow shipwreck victims would soon freeze to death unless something was done. Faced with the horror of having coaxed his beloved into an apparent death trap, he came up with a desperate plan. To save themselves, he and his companions would roll up in a blanket and lie down together beside the stern rail. The mate hoped the freezing spray would form a protective shell of ice on the outside of the blanket. This it did, but the ice grew much thicker than he had anticipated. All night the sea continued to douse the three until they were entombed in a layer of ice several inches thick.

Under the suffocating weight of the ice, the mate and his girl lost consciousness, and by morning, the deckhand believed he was the only one left alive. Slashing at the ice with a small knife and using his bleeding hands as hammers, he managed to free himself. When he was strong enough to stand, the sailor saw that the tide had gone out and a narrow bridge of exposed rock now connected the schooner with the shore. So, bloodied and nearly frozen, he dropped down off the deck and stumbled off toward the Owls Head Light, which he could see shining through the storm. Overwhelmed by cold and exhaustion, he made the last part of the journey crawling on his hands and knees. But he eventually reached his destination, and in the warm kitchen of the keeper's dwelling, he told his incredible story.

The keeper had little hope of finding anyone alive aboard the schooner; nevertheless, he organized a rescue party and headed for the wreck. There the rescuers found a man and a woman locked in a lovers' embrace and frozen in a solid block of ice. It took picks, chisels, knives, and several strong men to free the pair. Everyone was sure they were dead; even so, an attempt was made to revive them.

Hurried ashore to a home near the lighthouse, their seemingly lifeless bodies were treated with cold-water baths and constant massage. In two hours the woman regained consciousness. An hour after that, the mate also showed signs of life. It took the two several months to recover from their ordeal, but by June they were strong enough to stand together in front of a preacher and pronounce their vows.

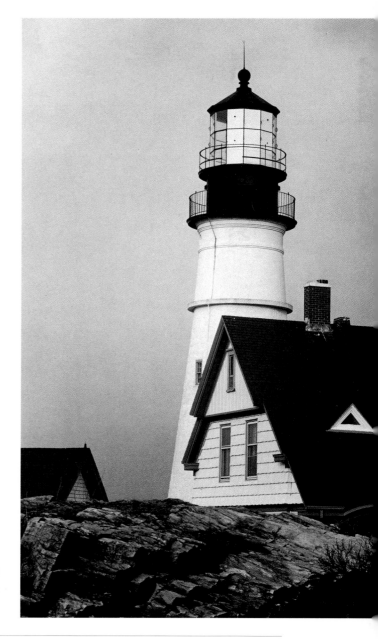

Ironically, the sailor, whose grueling trek through the storm had brought help and saved the lovers from certain death, never fully recovered from his adventure. He did not go to sea again and lived out his life on waterfronts of towns near Owls Head. He never tired of telling strangers about his struggle in the blizzard of 1850, and, coincidentally, about the frozen lovers of Owls Head.

Tower and dwellings rise behind ramparts of rock at Portland Head, Maine.

CURTIS ISLAND LIGHT
Camden, Maine - 1836

Pleasure sailors and schooner captains who see the fixed green light on Curtis Island know that the charming town of Camden and its well-maintained harbor lie just beyond. Camden, with its scenic mountains and ocean vistas, is one of the most popular tourist centers along the Maine coast. But it was once a busy port and home to dozens of merchant-ship captains who roamed the world in search of a profit. For many of these sea traders the light shining from atop the Curtis Island tower, fifty-two feet above the water, was an especially welcome sight. It offered them their first glimpse of home, often after an absence of several years.

Curtis Island is named for Cyrus Curtis, a Mainer with a keen business mind and a penchant for publishing. Curtis became world famous and fabulously wealthy as a publisher of family magazines such as *The Saturday Evening Post.* Curtis spent a few of his millions in Camden, maintaining a lavish estate, anchoring an enormous luxury yacht—converted into a warship during World War II—in the town's harbor, and donating land and buildings for a yacht club and other public facilities. In return for his largesse, citizens gave Curtis's name to the island where the Camden Harbor light stood.

Until then, the island had been known as Negro Island. No one is certain how the island came to be called that, but there is a legend concerning the name. It is said that one of the first settlers to arrive on this pristine coast brought with him a black deckhand. When it came time to divide up the land, the deckhand, perhaps recently freed from slavery, said he would take the lonely island as his parcel and leave the mainland to the whites. No one remembers the man's name, but for a time, at least, he was a wealthy man—he had a whole island to himself.

Since it is located on the south (seaward) side of the island, the light is difficult to see from land. A view can be had, however, by turning toward the water at the Camden Post Office and following Penobscot Avenue. The lighthouse will appear on the left as you approach the end of the road. For more precise directions and suggestions on how to see the light, ask at the visitors' center beside Camden Harbor.

Several schooners, such as the Stephen Tabor and the Roseway, operate out of the harbor during warm-weather months. They offer sailing tours of a week or more in length. The most charming way to see Curtis Island Light may be from the deck of one of these wonderful old vessels.

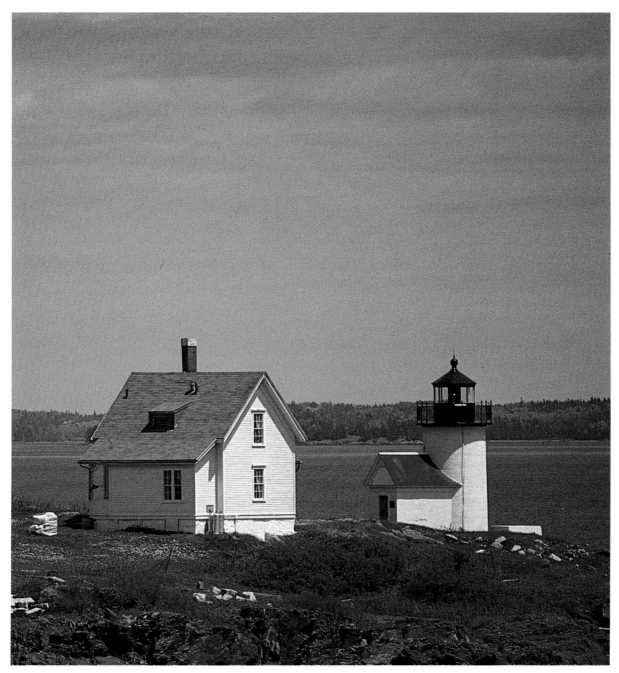

Shown here in a summer view, Curtis Island Lighthouse stands at the entrance to Camden Harbor. The island is named for Cyrus Curtis, founder of The Saturday Evening Post. *In 1993, the Curtis Island keeper's house received a striking, new red roof. The red roof makes a good day mark, especially with snow on the ground.*

BROWNS HEAD LIGHT AND GOOSE ROCKS LIGHT
Vinalhaven Island, Maine - 1832, 1890

In 1603 an obscure English mariner and explorer named Martin Pring dropped the anchor of his fifty-ton ship *Speedwell* in a narrow passage between two medium-size islands at the mouth of the Penobscot Bay. Pring saw foxes bounding and playing on the shore, so he named these the Fox Islands. Two hundred years ago the Massachusetts Legislature changed the name of Pring's islands to Vinalhaven and North Haven. But the name of the channel separating them remained the Fox Islands Thorofare, and that is what it is called today.

Each summer, thousands of pleasure craft sail through this passage, so it is a "thoroughfare" in fact as well as in name. Marking the western entrance of the Fox Islands Thorofare is Browns Head Light, built in 1832 and renovated twenty-five years later. Marking the eastern entrance, and warning boaters away from a dangerous shoal, is Goose Rocks Light, built in the caisson or "spark-plug" style in 1890. The tower at Browns Head stands thirty-nine feet above the water and displays a fixed white light with two red sectors. The Goose Rocks tower stands fifty-one feet above the water and displays a fixed white light with one red sector.

For seventy-three years, until the light was automated in 1963, the Goose Rocks Lighthouse was considered a "stag" station. With its base awash in salt water and the occupants confined to a few small rooms inside the tower, this lighthouse was no place for a family. The keepers could see their wives or children only when they were off duty and could go ashore for a visit, perhaps on a three-days-on—three-days-off schedule.

Vinalhaven Island can be reached by car ferry from Rockland. For ferry information and reservations call (207) 863–4421. The way from the Vinalhaven ferry slip to the Browns Head Light is complicated, so you should ask directions once you reach the island. If the person you ask speaks with a thick Maine accent, and that is a language unfamiliar to you, then perhaps you should ask someone else. The simplest way to reach the light may be to rent a taxi.

Goose Rocks Lighthouse cannot be reached by land. It can, however, be seen from certain points on Vinalhaven Island. Bring binoculars for viewing the light as well as the marvelous array of wildlife inhabiting the island.

HERON NECK LIGHT

Green Island (South of Vinalhaven), Maine - 1854

As is the case with many communities along the Maine coast, Vinalhaven has a population that comes in and goes out like the tides. Shorefront cottages and grand captains' houses often stand cold and empty much of the year. Then, usually on the weekend closest to July 4, the shutters come down, the lights go on, and these big, old houses are lonely no more. Vinalhaven's year-round population is only about 1,000, but it may swell to several times that in the summer.

Among those who live on the island in February as well as July are a considerable number of fishermen, most of them operating out of Carvers Harbor. For more than 135 years, fishermen running in off the sea toward this bustling port have been guided by the Heron Neck Light on Green Island, just south of Vinalhaven. A fixed red light with one white sector, it marks the western entrance to the Penobscot Bay as well as the approaches to Vinalhaven.

Built in 1854 on the brink of a high cliff, this lighthouse has a magnificent setting. The tower (the attached dwelling burned in 1989) stands on open ground facing south toward the Atlantic. Behind the station, a dense forest of tall spruce walls it off from the north.

The reddish-brown granite cliffs below the lighthouse serve as a reminder of the industry that brought prosperity to Vinalhaven a century ago. Huge quantities of this handsome granite were quarried on the island and shipped to cities along the East Coast. Countless banks, train stations, courthouses, and office buildings have solid chunks of Vinalhaven in them.

Since it is located on an island detached from Vinalhaven proper, this attractive lighthouse is very hard to reach. It is probably most easily seen from the air or water. Arrangements for a visit can sometimes be made in Carvers Harbor. A state-operated ferry service links Vinalhaven to Rockland on the mainland; for schedules and information, call (207) 596–2202.

ROCKLAND BREAKWATER LIGHT
Rockland, Maine - 1888

During the nineteenth century, Maine began to produce and ship prodigious quantities of lime to markets all over America. Much of this lime, used by construction crews for making mortar and cement, passed through the mid-coast port of Rockland. Because Rockland had a relatively unprotected harbor, lime freighters lying at anchor there were endangered by waves rolling in from the broad Penobscot Bay.

To correct this problem and make the harbor safe, the town decided to build a long stone breakwater extending nearly a mile from Jameson's Point out into the bay. But no sooner had construction begun than the breakwater itself became a significant navigational obstacle. On foggy days especially, near misses by ships sailing in and out of the harbor were common. So workers erected a light, moving it a little farther seaward with the completion of each new section of breakwater. This "traveling" lighthouse served effectively as a temporary measure. Then, when the breakwater was finished, the government established a permanent light station at the far end.

Rebuilt along with the breakwater in 1902, the station consists of a white, square tower and an attached two-story keeper's dwelling. The station has a powerful foghorn, and its lens, located thirty-nine feet above the water, throws out a bright white flash every five seconds.

Built in 1888, Rockland Breakwater Light marks the end of a mile long stone jetty.

Rockland Breakwater Light is reflected in the soft purple of Rockland Harbor at sunset.

From U.S. 1, turn toward the water onto Waldo Avenue just north of downtown Rockland. Then turn right onto Samoset Road. Samoset Road is only about one half mile long, and when you reach its end, the breakwater will be just ahead and on your right. You can also get an excellent view of the lighthouse from the decks of the car ferries that serve North Haven (207–867–4441), Vinalhaven (207–863–4421), and Bass Harbor islands (207–244–3254).

While in Rockland, be sure to stop at 104 Limerock Street and see the Shore Village Museum, generally regarded as having the most comprehensive display of lighthouse materials in the New England area. The array of magnificent Fresnel lenses includes the second-order lens from Minots Ledge and the classic fourth-order lens from Baker's Island Lighthouse. Hear the deep moan of fog horns, and feel the weight of the old fog bell, once rung for exhaustive hours in warning. For more information call (207) 594–0311.

OWLS HEAD LIGHT
Rockland, Maine - 1826

Sailors headed for Rockland sometimes swear they can see the face of a giant bird sculpted by nature into the rocks of the promontory southeast of the town. They point at two caves forming the eyes and rocky outcroppings giving the great bird a nose and beak, as well as a pair of owlish ears. "There it is," they say. "Can't you see it?" Others laugh and say they see nothing on Owls Head but rocks—and a Coast Guard light station.

Built during the presidency of John Quincy Adams to guide lime freighters into Rockland Harbor, the lighthouse is one of the oldest in New England. Unlike most other old light stations, its tower has never been pulled down and rebuilt. The tower is only about twenty feet tall, but because it rises from a high promontory, its fixed white light shines from about 100 feet above the water. A fifth-order Fresnel lens focuses the light, which can be seen from about sixteen miles at sea.

The mysterious owl in Owls Head has seen many strange happenings. Consider, for instance, the saga of the frozen lovers described in the introduction to this chapter.

In 1745 a party of Indians on Owls Head captured Thomas Sanders, a young English sailor. But Sanders proved a bit too quick for his captors. He asked them to loan him a musket so he could "shoot some ducks." In a truly extraordinary display of gullibility, the Indians obliged, and Sanders, brandishing the borrowed musket, escaped into the woods.

In the early summer of 1757, a fleet of thirty canoes brought a large Penobscot

Its tower only about 20 feet tall, Owls Head is Maine's stubbiest lighthouse. Legends concerning it abound, however, and in this sense, the little lighthouse can be said to be many-storied.

Mariners swore they could see the head and the tufted ears of a great stone owl on this point. Since 1826, Owls Head Light has helped keep ships away from the dangerous rocks here.

Indian war party to Owls Head. A small force of white soldiers fought off the attackers and, turning the tables on the Indians, scalped two of them.

As they sailed out of Rockland Harbor on November 9, 1844, sailors on the fine new brig *Maine* may have looked back at Owls Head and argued over whether, indeed, it resembled the head of an owl. None of them would ever get another chance to resolve the question. This was the *Maine's* maiden voyage and also its last voyage. The *Maine* never arrived in New Orleans, where it was scheduled to deliver a load of Rockland lime. As if plucked from the seas by a giant predatory bird, the brig disappeared, along with its crew of nine. Then, three years later, a ship dropped anchor in Rockland Harbor. On board were a mahogany chest, a ship's atlas, and a navigation book, which local people swore belonged to members of the *Maine's* crew. According to the captain of the visiting vessel, three Portuguese sailors had left these items behind when they jumped ship in Vera Cruz. No further traces were ever found of the *Maine* or her crew.

During the 1930s, Owls Head Light had a dog as an assistant keeper. The dog, a sharp-eared springer spaniel named Spot, barked loudly whenever he heard a ship. He would also ring the fog bell by pulling on the rope with his teeth. It is said Spot once saved the Matinicus mail boat from smashing into the Owls Head rocks. A blizzard had cut visibility to near zero and frozen up the fog bell so that it could not be rung. But mail-boat captain Stuart Ames heard the dog barking and managed to bear off from the rocks in time to avert disaster.

From U.S. 1 in Rockland take Route 73 south for about two miles. Turn left, drive two and one-half miles, and a few hundred yards past the Owls Head Post Office, turn left again onto Lighthouse Road. After less than a mile you will reach a barrier and a small dirt parking lot. You cannot see the lighthouse from the parking lot, but don't be discouraged. Walk around the barrier and continue on foot. Just ahead is one of the grandest views and most charming lighthouses you are ever likely to enjoy. But take care, especially with children, since the cliffs on either side of the road are steep.

WHITEHEAD LIGHT
Off Tenants Harbor, Maine - 1807

Built by order of President Thomas Jefferson in 1807, Whitehead is one of the oldest lighthouse stations in Maine. It also produced one of the earliest Lighthouse Service scandals, when the station's very first keeper, Ellis Dolph, perhaps dissatisfied with his low government salary, decided to make a little money on the side. The scandal surfaced when officials noticed that the Whitehead lamps seemed to have an insatiable appetite for whale oil. An inspector sent up from Boston to investigate discovered that the lamps were not the problem. He found citizens all over Thomaston and Rockland who had purchased oil from Dolph. These people had been told the oil came from a surplus supply belonging to the keeper, but this was not the case. Instead, Dolph dipped it right out of the government tank beside the lighthouse tower at Whitehead. Dolph was fired but apparently was not prosecuted for his "double dipping."

Rebuilt by the Lighthouse Board in 1852, the station now consists of a round granite tower approximately seventy-five feet above the water and an attached red-brick service building. It guides mariners with a green light that occults once every four seconds.

Sailors often count themselves lucky to see the Whitehead Light at all. This stretch of the Maine coast is one of the foggiest places in America. The light station is socked in by fog an average of once every five days for a total of nearly 2,000 hours per year. For this reason, an effective fog bell was always considered indispensable here. In fact, the bell was in such constant use that keepers rigged up a mechanical device to ring it automatically. This contraption was powered by the waves and tides and struck the 2,000-pound bell four times each minute with a fifteen-pound hammer. The constant ringing must have given the keepers some terrible headaches.

The lighthouse cannot be reached by land and is most easily viewed from the air or water. The third-order Fresnel lens from the tower is now on display at the Shore Village Museum in Rockland, Maine.

More accessible is the Marshall Point Light just outside Port Clyde, a charming fishing village. From U.S. 1 at Thomaston, take Route 131 through St. George and Tenants Harbor to Port Clyde. Erected in 1832 and rebuilt in 1858, the tower is about thirty feet tall and is connected to land by a bridge. It displays a fixed white light.

A shrouded sentinel, Whitehead Lighthouse stands on one of the foggiest stretches of coast in the United States. Its foghorn was once powered by the tides.

PEMAQUID POINT LIGHT
Pemaquid Point, Maine - 1827

Old sailors enjoy pointing out that "the fog itself is not a problem; it's what you can't see because of the fog that gets you into trouble—like ships or shoals." Or big storms.

On the afternoon of September 16, 1903, the fishing schooner *George Edmunds* was plowing through a thick fog several miles off the Maine coast. Suddenly, like a curtain rolling up at the start of a drama, the fog lifted. Captain Willard Poole could see now, and he was glad enough of that. But he did not like what he saw. The fog had hidden from him a bank of angry black clouds, and the storm was now bearing down on the *Edmunds*. Alarmed, the captain gave the order to make for land.

Poole could see the flash of Pemaquid Point Light and steered directly for it. He knew the calm waters of John's Bay lay just beyond the light. But the *Edmunds* would never reach the bay. Sailors familiar with the area knew that a course for John's Bay must be "shaped" so as to avoid a point of land just west of the lighthouse. Poole tried to do this but misjudged his course by about 1,000 feet. The *Edmunds* struck hard on the rocks and was quickly dashed to fragments by the stormy sea. The captain drowned, and only two of his thirteen crew members survived the disaster.

Thanks to the lighthouse, active since 1827, only a few such wrecks have

Ocean waves have carved images of themselves on these unique formations. Shown here catching the last rays of sunlight on a summer day, the Pemaquid Point Lighthouse warns mariners not to sail on these rocks.

occurred off Pemaquid. The original lighthouse was built during the presidency of John Quincy Adams for $4,000. The Lighthouse Board saw fit to rebuild the tower in 1857 and fit it with a fourth-order Fresnel lens. The rubblestone tower is only thirty-eight feet tall, but since it sits on a high cliff, the light flashes out over the sea from a point seventy-nine feet above the water.

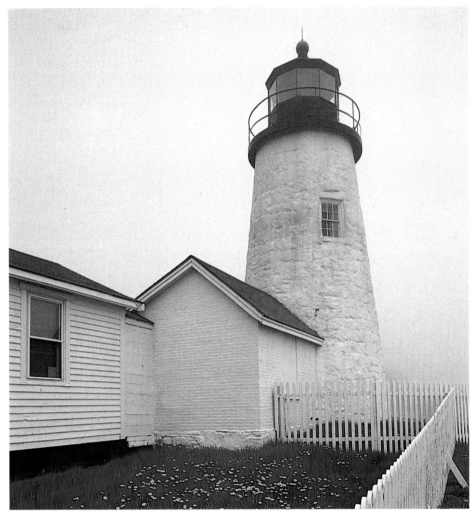

Dandelions decorate the fenced yard of the Pemaquid Point Lighthouse keeper's dwelling, now a museum filled with maritime and lighthouse artifacts.

Turn south off U.S. 1 at Damariscotta and follow Route 130 for approximately sixteen miles to the Pemaquid Point parking lot. Sculpted by nature, the extraordinary rock formations here remind some of water thrown up by the pounding surf and about to run back into the sea. At the lighthouse, the keeper's dwelling now houses the fascinating "Fishermen's Museum." For more information call the museum at (207) 677–2494. The museum is open by appointment in winter; call (207) 677–2726.

HENDRICKS HEAD LIGHT
Boothbay Harbor, Maine - 1829

One March, not long after the Civil War, a late-winter's blizzard blasted the coast of Maine. The storm wrecked many ships. One of them, a hapless schooner, struck a shoal not half a mile from the Hendricks Head Lighthouse.

The frantic keeper found he could not launch the station's rescue dory in the pounding surf. Unable to assist the schooner's desperate crew, he was forced to stand by helplessly while the shipwrecked sailors froze to death in the ship's rigging. The keeper did build a bonfire to give the sailors the comfort of knowing that they had at least been seen. He could do nothing else.

The disconsolate keeper was sure that all aboard the schooner had perished. Then he spotted what he later described as "a curious bundle tossing lightly in the thundering sea." The keeper and his wife managed to pull the bundle, a feather mat-

Hendricks Head Lighthouse was awaiting significant renovation when this photograph was taken in 1875. The sailing vessel on the left may be a supply ship bringing materials for reconstruction of the tower and dwelling. (Courtesy U.S. Coast Guard)

tress, out of the surf. To their amazement, they heard cries coming from within the ice-encrusted mattress. Chipping away at the ice and ripping open the mattress, they discovered a small sea chest and, inside that, a baby—frightened but very much alive. Accompanying the child was a note from the schooner's captain and his wife explaining that they had "committed [their daughter] into God's hands." The disaster hadn't been total after all.

Commissioned in 1829, the Hendricks Head Lighthouse stands on a rocky point on Southport Island overlooking the mouth of the Sheepscot River. The light helped guide fishing boats into Boothbay Harbor and freighters along a dangerous stretch of coast south of the powerful Seguin Island Lighthouse.

In 1875 the original structure was replaced by a forty-foot brick tower and separate, wooden keeper's dwelling. A bell tower was added in 1890. The government decommissioned the light in 1933 during the Great Depression and eventually sold the land to private interests. The old lighthouse has been restored to near-perfect condition by the current owners, who use it as a year-round residence.

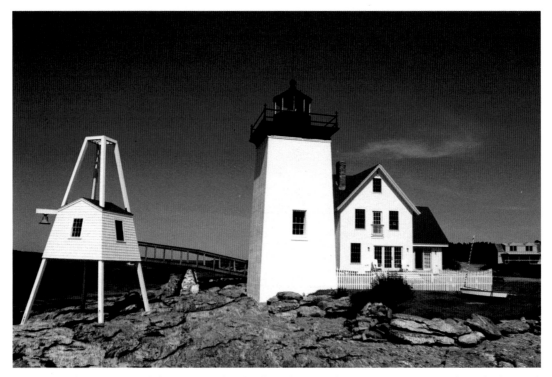

The square, brick tower and detached wooden dwelling shown in this contemporary view of Hendricks Head Lighthouse replaced the original lighthouse in 1875. (Courtesy of Ben Russell)

From U.S. Highway 1 turn toward the ocean on Route 27 and follow it for ten miles to Lakeside Drive. Turn right onto Lakeside and, after about 2 1/2 miles, turn right again and cross a bridge onto Southport Island. The lighthouse is located on Beach Road approximately 3 miles straight ahead. The lighthouse is on private property, so please respect the rights of the owners. Nearby are Boothbay and Boothbay Harbor, both well known for their seafood and as haunts for droves of summer visitors.

SEGUIN ISLAND LIGHT
Seguin Island, Maine - 1795

With its lantern located 186 feet above the sea and fitted with a powerful first-order Fresnel lens, the Sequin Island Light ranks as one of America's foremost lighthouses. On clear evenings its fixed white light has been seen some forty miles at sea. One of the nation's oldest light stations, it has the only first-order lens still operational in Maine. George Washington himself gave the order to build the first tower here in 1795, and Congress appropriated $6,300 to see the job done right.

But despite the money available, considerable for the time, the tower was constructed of wood. By 1819 the sea and the weather had completely dilapidated the lighthouse, and it had to be rebuilt. This time the builders used stone and billed the government less than $2,500.

The original wooden tower lasted less than twenty-five years, but it stood up to Seguin's harsh weather a lot longer than Count John Polersky, the station's first keeper. Born to a noble family in Alsace, Polersky immigrated to America, where

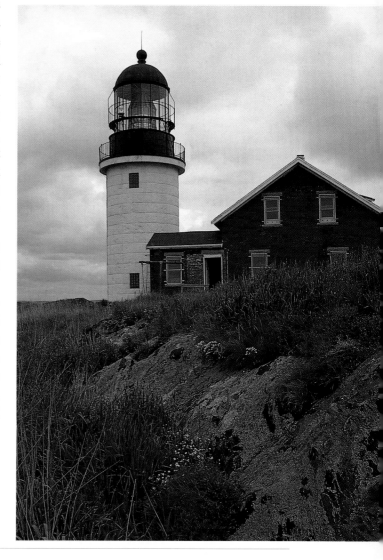

he served as a major in Washington's Continental Army. Polersky's salary was set at $200 per year, not a handsome income for a European nobleman nor even for a Revolutionary War officer. Polersky pleaded for a raise but was repeatedly turned down. Meanwhile, the station's cruel weather turned his home into a shack, smashed and sank his three boats, tore apart his barns, beat down his gardens, and left his health in ruins. After five years on the island, during which time he faithfully tended the light, Polersky died.

Located in the mouth of the Kennebec River, the Seguin Light station stands on historic ground. Two small ships, the *Gift of God* and the *Mary and John,* dropped anchor near the island in 1607. They had brought settlers who hoped to establish the first English colony in North America. The settlers planted a flag and built a small town on the banks of the Kennebec. But hunger, hardship, and a terrible Maine winter killed

The Friends of Seguin Island, a nonprofit corporation, now maintains and preserves the lighthouse. There are monthly boat trips from the Maine Maritime Museum, in Bath, during the summer. For current information write Friends of Seguin Island, Box 438, Georgetown, ME 04548.

many and caused the survivors to abandon the colony and sail back home to England. No doubt, the would-be colonists wished they had never seen Seguin Island.

Even the Indians, who gave Seguin its name, were wary of the island. Seguin is an English corruption of an Indian word loosely translated as "place where the sea vomits." Considering that Indian fishermen had to fight the choppy seas at the mouth of the Kennebec in flimsy canoes, they may have intended to describe Seguin as the place where they themselves vomited.

The wind and weather have made their mark on Seguin's oil house.

Located on an island about two miles from Popham Beach at the mouth of the Kennebec River, the lighthouse cannot be reached by land. But the tower and light can be viewed at a distance from Popham Beach. Turn onto Route 209 off U.S. 1 at Bath. During the summer, tour boats from Boothbay Harbor offer views of the light. The Maine Maritime Museum, in Bath, runs tour boats to the island throughout the summer. Visitors may also reach the island by Echo Helicopter (207–775–5440). A magnificent view is afforded from the rocky bluffs and tower. An excellent small museum (207–371–2152) depicts the history of the island and its keepers through vintage photographs and maritime artifacts.

By taking short side roads off Route 209 along the way to Popham Beach, you can also see Perkins Island Light and Squirrel Point Light. Both built in 1898, these lighthouses mark the Kennebec River channel.

The Squirrel Point Light (left) and Perkins Island Light (right), both built in 1898, guard the channel of Maine's legendary Kennebec River. Navy ships built by the Bath Iron Works upriver sail down to the sea through this channel.

PORTLAND HEAD LIGHT
South Portland, Maine - 1791

The nation's first Congress under the Constitution convened in New York City in 1789. Its initial order of business was the Bill of Rights, but the ink was barely dry on that honorable document before Congress turned its attention to lighthouses. President George Washington had a particular interest in ocean and river commerce and wanted all lighthouses and other navigational aids brought under the wing of the new federal government. On August 7, 1789, Congress obliged the president by passing one of the earliest federal laws, an act setting up a "Lighthouse Establishment" or, as it would later be known, Lighthouse Service.

Under provisions of the act, the government took over ownership and responsibility for eleven lighthouses along the nation's Atlantic shores, including the famed Boston Light, built in 1716. The list would have numbered an even dozen except that construction of the important Portland Head Light, begun two years earlier by the Commonwealth of Massachusetts, was still far from complete. Massachusetts had fallen on hard financial times and could no longer afford to pay for the project. An impatient Washington told Secretary of the Treasury Alexander Hamilton to get the project moving. Hamilton squeezed $1,500 out of Congress, only enough money to build a tower with fieldstone dragged to the construction site by oxen, but by late in 1790 the tower stood ready, its lantern nearly 100 feet above the water. The builders did their job well. The tower has survived almost 200 years of pounding by the persistent Atlantic. On January 10, 1791, keeper Joseph Greenleaf put a match to the station's lamps, and the lantern where he stood has rarely been darkened since.

Driven for more than a century by a second-order Fresnel lens (now replaced

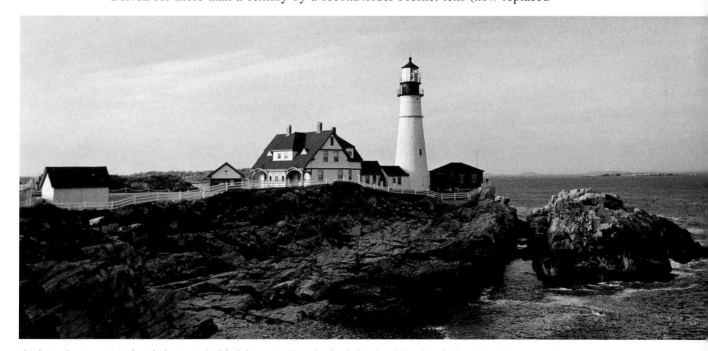

Perhaps the most visited and photographed lighthouse in New England, Portland Head Light has shone from countless posters, calendars, bank checks, and postcards.

by a rotating, airport-style beacon), the flashing light on Portland Head has guided countless vessels to safe harbor. One that never made it, however, was the steamer *Bohemian.* Bound from Liverpool, England, to America with 218 passengers, many of them immigrants, the *Bohemian* was just short of its goal when it met with disaster on February 22, 1868. Plowing through heavy seas and fog toward Portland, the steamer slammed into Alden's Rock a few miles south of the lighthouse. The rock tore through the *Bohemian's* tough iron hull as if through thin wooden planking, and people were soon jumping into lifeboats. The fully loaded Number Two boat broke away from its hoist and fell, dumping several dozen people into the winter sea. Most of them quickly froze to death or drowned. However, five other lifeboats reached shore safely, and riding in one of them was an Irish boy named John Fitzgerald. Boston would later know Fitzgerald as an astute politician.

Another wreck, some twenty years after the *Bohemian* disaster, brought the three-masted bark *Annie Maguire* right into the front yard of Portland Head Light's keeper Joshua Strout. Ironically, the *Maguire* was in deep financial and legal trouble,

and creditors planned to lay claim to the ship the moment it dropped anchor in Portland Harbor. The sheriff had asked Strout to be on the lookout for the vessel and notify authorities as soon as it sailed into sight. Strout's task proved much easier than he expected. On Christmas Eve, 1888, the bark appeared suddenly out of a storm and ran up onto the rocks only a few yards from Strout's front door on Portland Head. Drawn away from their Christmas tree by the collision, which sounded to them like an earthquake, the Strout family ran outside and pitched in to rescue the *Maguire's* fifteen-man crew. Later, the sheriff was able to serve papers on the beleaguered ship right there at the lighthouse, but this accomplished little for the new owners. The *Maguire* was so beaten up by the wreck that she later sold at auction for only $177.

Portland Head Light was automated on August 7, 1989, during the Lighthouse Service Bicentennial celebration. The keeper's dwelling was given to the town of Cape Elizabeth.

Workmen prepare to lower part of the light apparatus as the Portland Head Lighthouse is automated in 1989.

One of the most visited and most often photographed lighthouses in America, the Portland Head Light stands adjacent to Fort Williams State Park near South Portland. From U.S. 1, take Highway 1A, Route 77, and Shore Road. Turn left into Fort Williams Park and follow signs to the lighthouse parking lot. The Portland Head Museum is now open daily until November first, 10:00 A.M.–4:00 P.M., and on weekends until December 20. For current information call the museum at (207) 799–2661.

OTHER PORTLAND HARBOR LIGHTS
1837, 1897 and 1905

The approaches to the harbor of Maine's largest city are so rocky and dangerous that dozens of navigational markers are needed to guide ships through safely. On their way into the harbor, sailors encounter several major lights. In fact, Portland, Maine, is one of only a few cities anywhere that can boast four lighthouses. Sailing northwest out of the Gulf of Maine and Casco Bay, mariners are greeted by Portland Head Light (see previous section) and Ram Island Light. Closer in they find their way with the help of the Spring Point Ledge and Portland Breakwater lights.

Built during the Teddy Roosevelt era, Ram Island Ledge Light warns ships away from one of America's deadliest ledges. Rocks lurk just beneath the surface near the island, and the list of ships they have damaged is long. The nineteenth-century schooners *Eliza Crowell, Laura Jane, W. C. Wellington, Hockomock, L. A. Johnson, Etna,* and *Tizar* all came to grief on or near the island. Tragically, so did many members of their crews. In 1902 the three-masted *Glenrosa* got lost in a fog and opened her hull on the ledge. The entire crew reached land safely, but the *Glenrosa* was so badly damaged that she later sold at auction for four dollars.

In operation continuously since its construction in 1905, the Ram Island Ledge Light made the Portland ship channel much safer. The station does its job with a seventy-seven-foot granite tower and a white light that flashes twice every ten seconds. A Fresnel lens makes the light visible from a distance of twelve miles.

Located at the end of a breakwater on the west side of the inner harbor, the Spring Point Ledge Light marks another outcropping of killer rocks. They stretch from old Fort Preble in South Portland to the very edge of the Portland ship channel, and like the Ram Island ledges, have torn or scarred the hulls of many vessels.

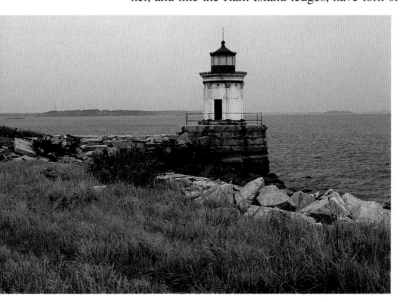

The Portland Breakwater Lighthouse suggests a tiny Greek temple, perhaps built in honor of Poseidon. Actually, the walls and fluted columns are of cast iron. The light has been painted and refurbished since this 1989 picture.

In 1832 they claimed the Rockland lime coaster *Nancy.* Strangely, the *Nancy* burned before she sank. Lime and water form a highly volatile mixture, and as soon as the sea started pouring through the *Nancy's* breached hull, the ship caught fire. The stubborn flames could not be doused, and the *Nancy* burned to the waterline.

But despite the destruction of the *Nancy* and other wrecks, nothing was done to mark the Spring Point Ledge until 1895, when Congress appropriated $45,000 to build a lighthouse there. Even then it took two years to get the light in operation. Whenever construction crews seemed about to complete the structure, storms swept in off the Atlantic to undo much of what had been accomplished. Keepers finally lit the station's lamps on May 24, 1897.

The lantern contains a fifth-order Fresnel lens that throws out both white and red flashes every five seconds. Ship pilots who see a white flash know they are safely inside the Portland channel. Those who see the red know they are drifting out into dangerous waters.

For most of its career this caisson-type lighthouse was completely surrounded by water. Since 1950, however, a 900-foot breakwater has linked the tower to the mainland. Built with granite blocks, each weighing several tons, the breakwater cost the government $200,000—more than four times as much as the lighthouse itself.

Another, much older, breakwater reaches into the harbor from the shore opposite Spring Point Ledge. Portland has always been vulnerable to nature's violence, and storms send giant waves hurdling in from Casco Bay. After a particularly destructive gale in 1831 smashed wharves, knocked down warehouses, and threw fishing boats and ships around like corks, the storm-weary residents of the town demanded and received the protection of a breakwater.

Extended and reinforced several times since it was completed in 1837, the Portland Breakwater eventually reached a length of nearly half a mile. A small wooden lighthouse was placed on its outer end in 1855 to keep ships from slamming into the breakwater stones. But it did not hold up well under the terrible beatings it took from storms and was replaced by a cast-iron tower in 1874. Although its lantern was permanently extinguished by the Coast Guard nearly fifty years ago, the iron tower still stands. Only thirteen feet tall and decorated in Greek style with false columns, the tower suggests a tiny Greek temple.

The little lighthouse is no longer far from shore. During World War II, the government filled in shallows around the breakwater to make room for dry docks and a shipyard where thousands labored around the clock turning out Liberty ships. Today, the lighthouse stands less than 100 feet from shore, its light no longer needed.

A typical "spark plug" light, the Spring Point Ledge Lighthouse was built in 1897.

Ram Island Ledge Light can be seen either from a boat or from Portland Head (see directions for Portland Head Light). For the Spring Point Ledge Light, follow Broadway through South Portland and turn right on Pickett Street. Then follow Fort Road until it ends at Fort Preble. For an excellent view of the light, climb the stone stairway over the wall of the fort. Portland Breakwater Light is also reached from South Portland. Check locally for directions.

CAPE ELIZABETH LIGHT
Cape Elizabeth, Maine - 1828

Like Matinicus Rock farther up the Maine coast, Cape Elizabeth once guided mariners with a pair of lights. In fact, the station was for many years known as "Two Lights." The two Cape Elizabeth towers, spaced about 300 yards apart, displayed a fixed light and a flashing light, respectively. When approaching the coast from the east, south, or west, a ship's position could be found quickly on a chart

The Cape Elizabeth Lighthouse has a distinctly nautical appearance. The keeper's home is now privately owned.

once a sailor had spotted the double lights. But today, only one light shines on the cape. In 1924 officials decided the second light was redundant and discontinued it.

The station has a long history. A forty-five-foot octagonal tower was erected on Cape Elizabeth in 1811 as a daymark, but it was of no use at all to ships' captains blinded by fog or darkness. So, under pressure from shipping interests, the government paid contractor Jeremiah Berry $4,250 to replace the daymark with two rubblestone towers. Working fast, Berry had both towers ready for service in less than five months, and their lamps were first lit in October 1828.

By 1874 both lighthouses had been all but destroyed by the weather and the sea, so they were pulled down and a pair of handsome cast-iron towers erected in their place. When the west light was discontinued in 1924, the lantern was removed from the tower. But the east tower still looks much the way it did more than a century ago. Standing on a high cliff and with a second-order Fresnel lens throwing out bursts of six rapid flashes every thirty seconds, it ranks as one of the most powerful lights in New England. Astoundingly, sailors can see the Cape Elizabeth Light from up to twenty-seven miles away.

Despite the power and effectiveness of the light, the rocky cape has continued, over the years, to claim ships. The schooner *Australia* struck rocks near the lighthouse during a blizzard on January 28, 1885. The keeper rescued two members of its crew. In addition to the *Australia*, the 286-ton bark *Tasmania*, the schooner *Abigail*, the schooner *Susan*, and many other ships were lost within sight of the station and its keepers.

On March 3, 1947, the coal freighter *Oakley L. Alexander* ran head-on into a storm so violent that the ship was broken in half. All thirty-two members of the ship's crew managed to clamber aboard the stern section, which continued to float. The accident took place more than eight miles from shore, but luckily for the crew, the wind was blowing toward land. The stern ended up on the rocks near the Cape Elizabeth Lighthouse. Using a lifesaving device called a Lyle gun, Coast Guardsman Earle Drinkwater fired a line over the stern and started hauling men ashore. Eventually, he was able to save the entire crew.

Portland Head and Cape Elizabeth lights can be visited in a single afternoon. From Portland Head return to Route 77 and turn left. Turn left again on Ocean House Road and enter Two Lights State Park, where signs will lead you to the Cape Elizabeth Light. Or, from U.S. 1A in South Portland, turn south onto Route 77 and follow it to Ocean House Road. Take your camera. The keeper's house at Cape Elizabeth is private property; however, there are good viewing areas nearby.

CAPE NEDDICK LIGHT
York, Maine - 1879

Just off Cape Neddick near the old town of York, Maine, lies a small barren island long known to fishermen as "the Nubble." Here the rocks seem to have boiled up out of the sea, and nature has created a sculpture garden by carving fantastic shapes into the exposed stone. Below the century-old lighthouse is a rock formation called the Devil's Oven. As if to warn the devil against cooking up anything too evil in his oven, a stone preacher's pulpit stands nearby. But the most famous formation on the Nubble is Washington's Rock. Visitors often say they can see a striking likeness of the nation's first president in the rock—but most agree that it takes some imagination.

Earlier visitors may have seen other faces in the stones of the Nubble. Perhaps Captain Bartholomew Gosnold, the English explorer who anchored beside the Nubble in 1602, saw the face of an Indian chief in the rock. Gosnold met here with coastal natives and later named the place Savage Rock. Following the mysterious destruction of the *Isidore* (described in the introduction to this chapter), local folk may have noticed the faces of phantom sailors in the Nubble's stones.

Probably no one has ever noticed a likeness of President Rutherford B. Hayes in the rocks of the island, but it was he who signed the order establishing a light station here in 1879. The government spent $15,000 building the lighthouse, keeper's dwelling, and support buildings.

The tower, though only forty feet tall, stands on the island's highest point; consequently, its light shines from an elevation of eighty-eight feet. The light flashes red every six seconds.

At least three weddings have been held at the Cape Neddick Lighthouse. One of these ceremonies was performed in the lantern room itself.

From U.S. 1 in York, take Route 1A to York Beach, turn right on Nubble Road, and proceed about one mile to Nubble Point. You can enjoy an excellent view of the lighthouse from the point, but do not attempt to cross over onto Nubble Island. The footing is dangerous and the tides may strand you on the island.

With sunlight still glinting from the upstairs windows of the keeper's house, the "Nubble" Lighthouse on Cape Neddick projects its first red flash of the night.

61

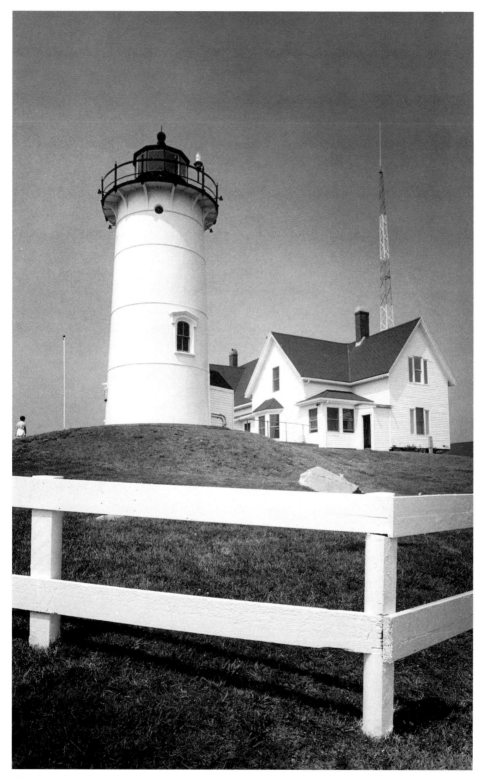

The brick-lined, iron tower of Nobska Lighthouse was built in 1876. It replaced an earlier tower, which had stood here for nearly 50 years. The keeper's house now serves as dwelling for a Coast Guard group commander.

CHAPTER THREE

LIGHTS OF FREEDOM'S SHORES

New Hampshire and Massachusetts

Lights of Freedom's Shores

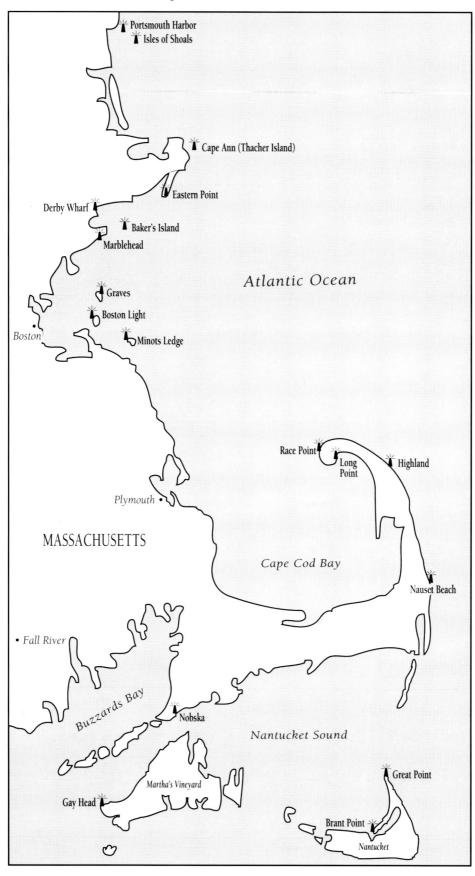

Portsmouth Harbor
Isles of Shoals

Cape Ann (Thacher Island)

Eastern Point

Derby Wharf

Baker's Island

Marblehead

Atlantic Ocean

Graves

Boston Light

Minots Ledge

Boston

Race Point

Long Point

Highland

Plymouth

MASSACHUSETTS

Cape Cod Bay

Nauset Beach

Fall River

Buzzards Bay

Nobska

Nantucket Sound

Great Point

Martha's Vineyard

Gay Head

Brant Point

Nantucket

On the night of April 18, 1775, Paul Revere watched for a signal from a makeshift lighthouse, the steeple of Boston's Old North Church. Soon a fellow patriot would raise a lantern in the steeple and send Revere riding hell-bent for Concord and Lexington and shouting his famous message: "The British are coming!" It is easy to imagine that while he waited, Revere occasionally took his eyes off the steeple to glance eastward toward the menacing British fleet that hovered just outside Boston Harbor. Looking in that direction he might have seen the beacon of the lighthouse on Little Brewster Island. Ironically, that light was probably far more important to the cause of American independence than the one Revere would shortly see in the Old North Church steeple.

ONE IF BY SEA

Built in 1716, the harbor lighthouse had guided countless thousands of trading ships to the Boston wharves and, in this way, contributed mightily to the prosperity of the colonies. That same prosperity had convinced the British that their upstart colonists should pay for the protection of King George's fleet and other expensive services rendered by the mother country. So Parliament decided to tax the colonies. American businessmen, who, to this day, have never smiled at the thought of taxes, responded hostilely even to the Parliament's penny-a-pound tax on tea. In Boston, a party of antitax demonstrators painted their faces, dressed up like Indians—another long-lived trait of Americans is their active sense of humor—and dumped a shipload of tea into the harbor. The British retaliated by blockading Boston with their fleet. After that, events moved swiftly. Massachusetts city dwellers and farmers started hoarding gunpowder and calling themselves Minutemen. People began to talk openly about independence from England, and having seen a light in a church steeple, Revere found himself riding through the night toward Lexington.

Incidentally, as a successful silversmith, Revere benefited considerably from the prodigious commerce made possible, in part, by the Boston Lighthouse. He and other Boston merchants had no aversion at all to taxing British ships to raise funds for upkeep of the light. By the time Revere made his ride, however, maintaining the light was no longer a problem. The British had taken over the lighthouse and were operating it themselves as a beacon for their ships.

To strike back at the blockading fleet, the Minutemen decided to put out the light. Early in July 1775, a small detachment of American troops landed on Little Brewster Island, removed the oil and lantern, and set fire to the lighthouse. To observers on the mainland the burning tower seemed a great torch "ascending up to Heaven." The flames confused gunners on the British warships, who tried but failed to blast the Minutemen out of the water as they retreated back to Boston.

But damage to the lighthouse was not as complete as the Americans might have hoped. The scorched walls of the tower had barely cooled before the British put workmen ashore on Little Brewster to begin repairs. A contingent of royal marines stood guard while the carpenters sawed lumber and pounded nails.

News of the rapidly progressing repair work soon reached Boston, where General George Washington had recently taken over command of the American army. Washington felt he could not allow the tower to be relighted and decided to send a second raiding party to the island. On July 30, 300 Continental soldiers, led by Major Benjamin Tupper, set out for Little Brewster in whaleboats. Aided by darkness, the Americans caught the redcoat marines completely by surprise and quickly defeated them. Once they had destroyed the work of the British carpenters and set fire to everything that would burn, the Continentals prepared to leave. But the tide had gone out, and their whaleboats were now stranded on dry land a long way from deep water.

Tupper knew that by now, the British were well aware of the raid on the lighthouse and soon would be mounting a counterattack. He ordered his men to bend their backs and shove the heavy whaleboats over the rocks and mud to the waterline. The major's concern proved well founded; just as the exhausted Americans reached the water with their boats, the British swooped down on them in a flotilla of armed launches. Tupper could see that his small force was outnumbered and feared that he and his men were now trapped on the island. But a flash and roar from the direction of nearby Nantasket Head quickly turned the tide of battle in favor of the raiders. An American artillery piece on Nantasket had opened fire and, scoring a direct hit on one of the British boats, caused the redcoats to panic and flee.

The Americans lost only one soldier in the fight, while their opponents suffered heavy casualties. The raid greatly pleased Washington, who saw it as proof that his lightly trained troops could carry out a well-disciplined maneuver under fire. Washington called the raiders "gallant and soldier-like" and praised them for so adroitly "possessing themselves of the enemie's post at the lighthouse."

WHEN IN THE COURSE OF HUMAN EVENTS

Although the harbor was now dark and unsafe for nighttime navigation, the British fleet did not leave. Several of the king's warships remained near the harbor entrance, harassing fishermen and threatening coastal towns and villages. The continued presence of enemy vessels in the harbor enraged Massachusetts patriots, especially Samuel Adams, the Boston firebrand who had more or less invented the American Revolution in the first place. Unable to stomach the sight of the British ships, Adams devised a plan to force them out of the harbor. The effectiveness of the gun at Nantasket

Head during Tupper's raid on the lighthouse may have suggested the scheme. The Americans would land troops on Nantasket Head and various strategic islands in the harbor, fortify them, and drive the blockaders away with artillery.

On June 13, 1776, only three weeks before the former colonies officially declared their independence from Britain, armed boats once more set sail from Boston and headed for the outer harbor. By dawn on the following day, the American gunners had their cannon ready, and the pounding began. The king's sailors woke up to a hot rain of shot and shell, and soon they had sails set and were racing for the high seas.

But before weighing anchor, one of the British ships put a landing party ashore on Little Brewster Island. The sailors hurriedly stacked gunpowder inside the lighthouse tower, lit a slow-burning fuse, and ran for their boats. While rowing back to their ship, they heard a thunderous explosion and watched the mortally wounded tower collapse into the sea. The Boston Light, it would seem, had few friends during the Revolutionary War.

DON'T GIVE UP THE SHIP

The lighthouse remained in ruins for seven years. Massachusetts Governor John Hancock, whose signature stands out from the others on the Declaration of Independence, asked his legislature to fund a new tower in 1780. The war with the British was not yet over, however, and the state had more pressing uses for its money. Almost three years passed before a light once more guided ships into Boston Harbor. By 1783, when keeper Thomas Knox finally lit the lamps in the new tower, the war had ended and a treaty had been signed with the British. People like Samuel Adams and Paul Revere would never again fume over having to pay taxes to the king. Instead they would grumble about paying them to their states, or later, to the new federal government for the upkeep, among other things, of lighthouses.

But the British would come back to Boston Harbor, close enough to Little Brewster Island for the rumble of cannon fire to rattle the windows of the Boston Lighthouse. During the War of 1812, keeper Jonathan Bruce and his wife, Mary, watched as the U.S. Navy ship *Chesapeake* took on the English warship *Shannon* at the very mouth of the harbor. Far-better-trained British gunners raked the *Chesapeake's* decks. Mortally wounded, Captain Lawrence gave his last order to the *Chesapeake* crew: "Don't give up the ship!" he cried. A few minutes later, however, having no choice but to surrender, his men did give up the ship.

Although the British won this and other nearby skirmishes during the war, keeper Bruce was never faced with having to "give up the lighthouse." The Boston Light survived this and later wars. Except during World War II, when it was extinguished to prevent German submarines from following the beacon into the harbor, the light has continued to shine to this day.

PORTSMOUTH HARBOR LIGHT
Portsmouth, New Hampshire - 1771

Colonial governments had very little money to spend on public works and were generally stingy with navigational improvements such as lighthouses. In New Hampshire, the first navigational light was so modest that it was not really a lighthouse at all. Each night, beginning in April 1771, a keeper hoisted a small lantern to the top of the flagpole at Fort William and Mary on the banks of the Piscataqua River. The costs of even this low-budget effort were paid, not by the colony, but by a levy on ships sailing in and out of Portsmouth Harbor. The name of the flagpole light keeper has been lost in the tides of history, but legend has it that he loaded gunpowder from the fort onto a wagon and sent it to the Minuteman army that battled the British at Bunker Hill. Perhaps he hoped that under an American government he might become keeper of a true lighthouse. And maybe he got his wish.

Eventually, the New Hampshire legislature did build a lighthouse on a narrow point of land beside the fort, but it is not clear when it went into operation. A wooden lighthouse tower already stood on the point in 1782 when Marquis de Lafayette, the famed Revolutionary War general, paid it a visit. A few years later, Lafayette's good friend and comrade-in-arms George Washington also visited the lighthouse.

Keeper Titus Salter, an old sea captain, must have spent days washing windows and floors, buffing metal fittings, and polishing the buttons on his coat after he learned, in 1789, that the president himself would be knocking on his door. And knock he did. Washington came and, despite the polished buttons, went away four days later with a less-than-enthusiastic opinion of the keeper. Soon, Salter started receiving uncomplimentary notes from Secretary of the Treasury Alexander Hamilton, whom Washington had placed in charge of the nation's "Lighthouse Establishment." It is difficult to say whether Salter was really doing a poor job of keeping the light or just had political differences with the administration, but by 1792 he was gone.

Hamilton replaced Salter with a man named Moses McFarland, who was extremely anxious to secure the position, even though it paid only $3.46 a week. The job was no prize. McFarland found he could barely feed his family of six on his low salary, and almost as serious a problem were the big guns at the adjacent fort, by then called Fort Constitution. Their thunder often cracked the walls and blew out the windows of the keeper's residence.

By 1804 both the residence and the tower had to be pulled down. In place of the old lighthouse, carpenters erected an octagonal tower. When complete, it stood eighty feet above the water, and its lantern contained thirteen spherical reflectors, each fourteen inches in diameter. Although made of wood, the new tower remained solid for nearly three-quarters of a century. It was finally torn down in 1877 and replaced by a cast-iron tower with a lantern fifty feet above mean sea level. This tower still stands today, its fourth-order Fresnel lens guiding ships with a flashing green light visible for twelve miles.

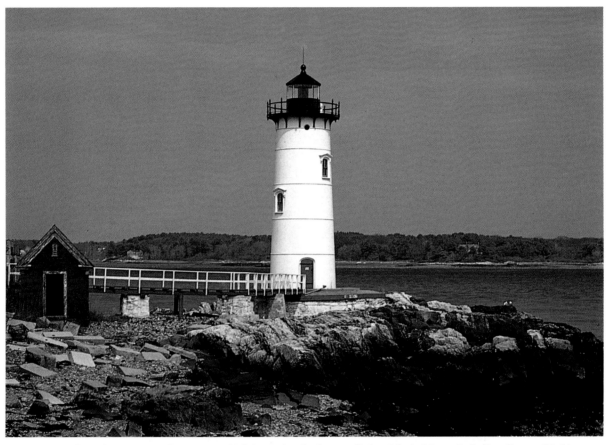

The Portsmouth Harbor, or Fort Constitution, Lighthouse has had many distinguished visitors, including George Washington, General Lafayette, and Daniel Webster. Before the Revolution, the stone fortress was known as Fort William and Mary.

From U.S. 1 in Portsmouth follow signs to Fort Constitution, or take Route 1B and then Wentworth Road to the fort, which is now part of a Coast Guard base. Most of the base is off limits, but the old colonial fort is open to the public. The best views of the light can be had from the fortress walls.

A ferry from Portsmouth carries visitors to the Isle of Shoals, location of another important New Hampshire lighthouse. Its light, flashing from a fifty-eight-foot granite tower, can be seen from fifteen miles at sea. The keeper's dwelling serves as a bed and breakfast.

ISLES OF SHOALS LIGHT
White Island, New Hampshire - 1821, 1859

Barren, rocky, swept by high winds, and pounded on all sides by towering waves, the Isles of Shoals are more a part of the ocean than of the land. Yet this tiny archipelago of islets, some of them no more than a few dozen yards across, was home to one of the earliest European settlements in North America. During the sixteenth century, fishermen flocked here like sea birds to exploit the giant schools of cod that teemed in the waters off the coast. Homes, churches, and packing sheds clung tenuously to the rocks—until the Atlantic threw up a storm to smash them. Survivors would then settle down to the task of rebuilding their homes and lives.

The Isles of Shoals have long attracted the adventurous and hardy of spirit. During the mid-1800s, Ralph Waldo Emerson visited the Appledore Hotel, a famed and gracious hostelry located on one of the Isles of Shoals' nine islands. Other guests included Nathaniel Hawthorne, William Mason, and John Greenleaf Whittier. The Old Appledore Hotel fell into ruin long ago; all but a few traces of it are gone. Yet

Barren rock and water provide a stark setting for Isles of Shoals Light Station, located several miles off Portsmouth, New Hampshire.

plenty of summer visitors still come here. A research station operated by Cornell University and the University of New Hampshire draws students and scientists who study the unique environment and wildlife of the islands. There is also a non-denominational church camp operated by the Unitarian-Universalists.

A lighthouse has stood on White Island—one of the Isles' more barren outcroppings— since 1821. The original stone tower stood eighty-two feet tall and served until just before the Civil War. In 1859 it was replaced by a shorter brick tower, its walls built two feet thick to help them survive the Atlantic's pounding waves. On more than one occasion, prodigious storms have swept the island, their thundering surf driving keepers into the tower for refuge. Today, the station is uninhabited, and its powerful light automated.

White Island, in the Isles of Shoals chain, is accessible only by private boat. The automated light station is closed to the public; however, it is possible to get an excellent view of the lighthouse from the Isles of Shoals Ferry. During warm-weather months the ferry leaves from Baker Wharf on Market Street in Portsmouth. For schedules and other information, call Isles of Shoals Steamship Company at (800) 441–4620 or (603) 431–5500.

CAPE ANN LIGHT
Thacher Island, Massachusetts - 1771

The Cape Ann Light station may once have saved the life of a president. Steaming home from Europe in 1919, the passenger liner *America* had on board a special guest, President Woodrow Wilson, returning from the Versailles Peace Conference, which officially ended World War I. Blinded by a heavy fog off the coast of Massachusetts, the *America*'s crew unknowingly had the big ship on a collision course with rocky Thacher Island just off Cape Ann. The fog was so thick that no one saw the lights of the island's twin lighthouse towers. Then a sailor heard the blast of a fog horn, and the captain ordered an emergency change of course—just in time to avert a disaster of truly historic proportions.

No one knows how many ships and lives have been saved by the Cape Ann station since it was established more than two centuries ago by the Bay Council of colonial Massachusetts. A few years before the start of the American Revolution, the council decided that too many good ships had been lost on the rocks of treacherous Thacher Island and that something must be done to warn mariners. The council determined to build not one, but a pair of lighthouses on the island. To secure land for the project, colonial officials bought the island from heirs of Reverend Anthony Thacher, who was, ironically, the first man known to have been shipwrecked there.

Thacher had suffered profound personal tragedy in 1635, when an August hurricane swept over the ship on which he and his family were passengers. The storm spared Thacher and his wife, throwing them up onto the barren shores of what later would be known as Thacher Island. But everyone else on the ship perished, including the four Thacher children. Partially to compensate the minister for his great loss, the colonial government gave him the island.

More than 135 years after the Thacher shipwreck, two stone towers stood on the island, their lanterns ninety feet above sea level. The colony hired as keeper a sea captain and notorious Tory named Kirkwood, who first lit the twin lamps on December 21, 1771. When the Revolution broke out a few years later, a party of Massachusetts Minutemen hustled Kirkwood off the island, and the lights were plunged into darkness until the end of the war.

Almost ninety years later, on the eve of another conflict—the Civil War—the Lighthouse Board rebuilt the old towers, raising them to a height of 124 feet above the rocks and 168 feet above the sea. When the work was completed in 1861, the board indicated the importance it placed on the Cape Ann Light station by fitting the lanterns of both towers with first-order Fresnel lenses. The northern light was discontinued in 1932 but has since been reactivated by the Thacher Island Association.

Occasionally, lighthouse keepers have been saved by their own lights. On Christmas Eve in 1865 the assistant keeper at Cape Ann fell seriously ill. The station's keeper, a wounded and crippled Civil War veteran named Bray, felt he had no choice but to take the sick man to the mainland, where he could receive proper medical attention. While Bray was ashore, the sea was brewing a storm. When the keeper headed back toward Thacher Island in his small boat, he found himself rowing into the teeth of a blizzard. It was snowing so hard that Bray had no idea whether he was pulling toward the island or toward the open sea. To miss the island meant almost certain death, and for a time, Bray thought that was exactly what he had done. Then he saw the glow of two familiar lights. The keeper's wife and children had struggled through deep snowdrifts to keep the lamps burning.

Bray pointed his boat toward the lights and put his back into the oars. Later, sitting at the table in his warm house and surrounded by his family, the keeper may have thought he had never tasted such a good Christmas dinner.

The twin lights on Thacher Island can be seen from the backshore areas of Gloucester on the mainland. Lands End in Rockport offers a particularly fine view. During the summer, some boat services in Rockland and Gloucester provide excursions to Thacher Island.

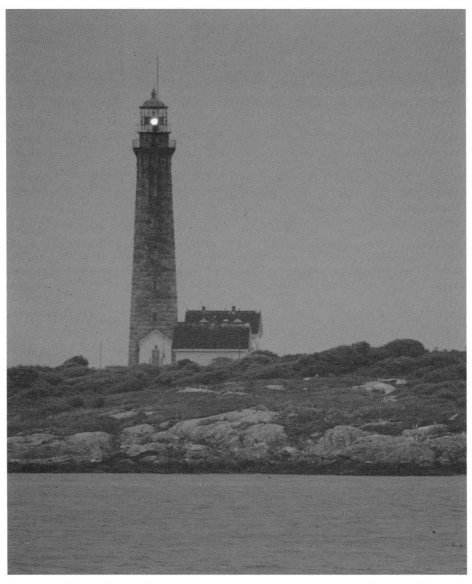

Cape Ann Light on Thacher Island warns mariners against repeating the misfortune of Reverend Anthony Thacher. In 1635, Thacher was shipwrecked on the island that now bears his name. Nearly three centuries later, the station likely saved President Woodrow Wilson from a similar fate.

EASTERN POINT LIGHT
Gloucester, Massachusetts - 1832

For more than 150 years the Eastern Point Light has guided Gloucester fishermen safely home from the sea. One of several lights near Gloucester, it marks the entrance to the town's bustling harbor. The tower and keeper's dwelling stand on the east side of the harbor on a long, rocky point of land forming a natural breakwater.

The first Eastern Point Lighthouse was built in 1832 but was replaced in 1890 by a larger brick tower and a wood-frame keeper's residence. Today, the station still looks much as it did a century ago, and the light continues to be seen each evening, its powerful beacon flashing once every five seconds.

According to several reliable witnesses, one of them a lighthouse keeper, a huge sea serpent visited Gloucester in 1817. Amos Story saw the monster and later testified that: "His head appeared shaped much like the head of a sea turtle and he carried his head from ten to twelve inches above the . . . surface of the water. His head . . . appeared larger than the head of any dog I ever saw . . . I should judge I saw 50 feet of him at least." Story later became keeper of the light built in 1823 on Ten Pound Island inside the Gloucester Harbor.

In Gloucester, take East Main Street to Eastern Point. Go through the gate marked Private and follow the paved road to a small dirt parking area at the breakwater. The lighthouse is closed to the public but can be viewed from the breakwater.

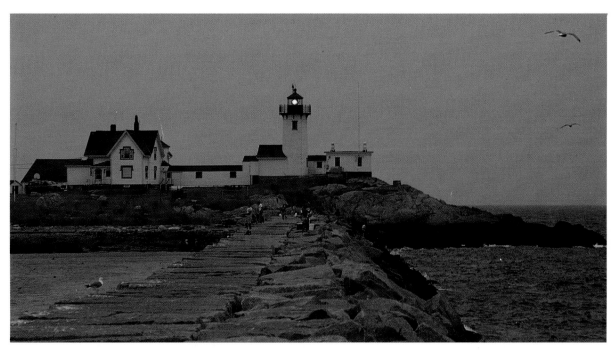

Eastern Point Light, flashing over the breakwater at Gloucester, marks the entrance to the harbor of this bustling fishing port.

DERBY WHARF LIGHT
Salem, Massachusetts - 1871

For more than 200 years ships reached Salem's inner harbor with little assistance from lights or other navigational aids. Eventually, the townspeople decided to extend a helping hand by hanging a small lantern on the side of an old warehouse. Finally, in 1870, the Lighthouse Board planned a system of three lighthouses to guide ships to Salem's busy wharves. The system, which included one light at Fort Pickering on Winter Island, another at Hospital Point in Beverly, and a third at the end of an extraordinary half-mile-long wharf in Salem, was late in coming. Ironically, Salem was already past its heyday as a shipping center by the time the lights were built and in operation.

Once known as "the Venice of the New World," Salem sent whole fleets of trading ships to India, China, and the West Indies. When these "Indiamen"

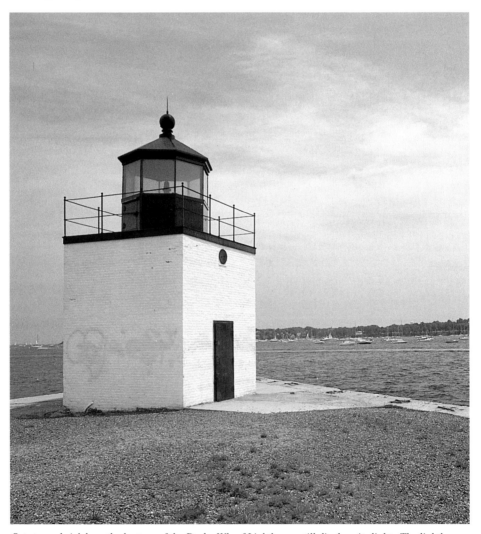

Set atop a brick box, the lantern of the Derby Wharf Lighthouse still displays its light. The lighthouse and the wharf are part of a national park devoted to Salem's rich maritime history.

returned, fortunes were made on the spices, sugar, molasses, coffee, tea, and chinaware that poured out of their holds. Salem's cleverest trader was Elias Derby, who was probably America's first millionaire. Although not a seaman himself, Derby knew how to make money on shipping ventures, and he swelled his profits by investing in construction of his enormous wharf.

Derby Wharf was itself proof of Salem's early commercial success. Along its east side, fifteen warehouses provided storage for the exotic goods flowing into the harbor. Stores and businesses of every variety rented space in the huge, two- and three-story wooden warehouses, while sailmakers, blacksmiths, coopers, and riggers also plied their trades there. Long lines of ships docked on the sheltered west side of the wharf.

By the spring of 1871 the wharf had its lighthouse, a twenty-five-foot-tall, square tower with a tiny lantern room at the top. The little light has an exceptionally varied career. During more than a century of service, it has burned both oil and acetylene as fuels and used electric lamps; it has displayed fixed white, flashing white, fixed red, and flashing red lights; it once had a sixth-order and later a fourth-order Fresnel lens. Today it displays a flashing red signal powered by a solar panel and reserve batteries.

From I-95 take Route 128 and Route 114 east to Salem and follow the brown National Park Service signs to the Salem Maritime National Historic Site. Start your tour at the visitors' center. You can easily spend an entire day in the old Custom House, Hawkes House, Derby House, and West India Goods Store, all of which have been carefully restored. You can walk to the lighthouse, which stands at the end of Derby Wharf well out into Salem Harbor. The walk along the old wharf is a treat. It is possible to imagine yourself an East Indian trader just in from Bombay with a load of spices.

BAKER'S ISLAND LIGHT
Salem, Massachusetts - 1798

During the War of 1812, civilian lighthouse keeper Joseph Perkins joined the U.S. Navy for a single thrilling afternoon. While keeping watch from his station on Baker's Island, Perkins spotted a pair of large British warships bearing down on the American frigate *Constitution,* which lay just outside of Salem Harbor. Outnumbered and outgunned, the captain of the *Constitution* wanted to avoid a battle and hoped to slip inside the harbor where there were shore guns to drive away the British. But he seemed unable to find a safe channel into the harbor. Instantly sizing up the situation, Perkins jumped into a boat, rowed out to the American ship, and offered his services as helmsman. Perkins knew the channels here as well as any sailor in Massachusetts. After piloting "Old Ironsides" to the safety of Salem Harbor and frustrating the British, Perkins returned to his worka-day chores at the Baker's Island Lighthouse.

Established in 1798, the Baker's Island light station originally displayed two lights. Like the original Matinicus Rock station in Maine, the lighthouse consisted of two towers connected by a keeper's dwelling. But during an early nineteenth-century economy drive, Treasury officials decided the island needed only one light and darkened the lantern in the second tower. Then, in 1817, the giant freighter *Union* slammed into the island, spilling tons of pepper and tin into the surf. Survivors of the wreck claimed they had mistaken the Baker's Island station, which now displayed only one light, for the single-towered Boston Light on Little Brewster Island.

Spurred by a public outcry, the government reactivated the second light, and Baker's Island remained a double-light station for another fifty years. Under orders from the Lighthouse Board, keepers finally snuffed out the second light in 1870, and it has remained dark ever since. But the other Baker's Island beacon still burns, more than a century after its companion became a "darkhouse." The light guides ships with alternating white and red flashes spaced about seven seconds apart.

Located on a small, isolated island in the Atlantic, this lighthouse is difficult to reach. It is most easily seen from the water or the air.

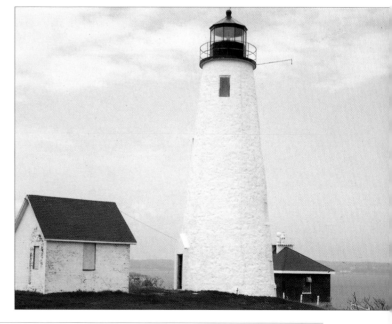

A single lighthouse tower now dominates rocky Baker's Island. The light in a companion tower was snuffed out in 1870.
(Courtesy U.S. Coast Guard)

MARBLEHEAD LIGHT

Salem, Massachusetts - 1836

Development has been an enemy of lighthouses, especially in this century. Newly constructed seaside hotels and other tall buildings have obscured beacons, forcing officials to move or even discontinue some light stations. Among the first lighthouses to be walled in by adjacent buildings was the small harbor light on Marblehead near Salem. Built in 1836 for $4,500, the squat Marblehead tower was not much taller than an ordinary house. It served effectively for many years, but by 1880, two- and three-story cottages had sprouted like weeds all around the station so that helmsmen trying to steer their vessels into Salem Harbor could no longer see the light at all.

As a temporary remedy, the keeper anchored a 100-foot mast firmly in the ground, and each night, he hoisted a lantern to the top. Eventually, this inadequate arrangement drew so many complaints from sailors that the Lighthouse Board approved a new tower for Marblehead. By 1895 work crews had completed the structure, a skeleton tower poised on eight iron legs. With its lantern 105 feet above the ground and 130 feet above the harbor, it raised the light far above the cottages that besieged the old lighthouse. The iron tower still stands today, exhibiting a fixed green light.

During the great New England Hurricane of 1938, the station's electric power failed, but keeper Harry Marden responded quickly to the emergency. Bringing his car to the tower, he hooked cables to the battery and kept the light burning.

From U.S. 1 take Route 114 to Marblehead. Turn right on Ocean Avenue, which ends near the lighthouse. A small park here provides benches and an excellent view of the water and of summer sunsets. The lighthouse is closed to the public.

A summer day ends with a splash of color at Marblehead Lighthouse. One of the few skeleton towers in New England, the lighthouse stands, as spiders do, on eight legs.

GRAVES LIGHT
Boston, Massachusetts - 1905

Gray and weather-streaked, the stone lighthouse tower on Graves Ledge looks very old, but its appearance is deceiving. Commissioned in 1905, it numbers among the few New England light stations established in this century. The Boston Harbor Light, built in 1716 on nearby Little Brewster Island, is almost 190 years older.

Although a relative newcomer, the Graves Ledge tower is nonetheless a testament to an old and proven way of building lighthouses. Beginning in 1903, stone-cutters at Cape Ann carefully shaped massive blocks of granite and loaded them onto the schooner *A. J. Miller* for shipment to the construction site, where masons painstakingly fitted them into place. Constantly lashed by the sea, work crews needed twenty-four months to lay down all of the forty-four courses of granite that lift the stone portion of the tower to a height of eighty-eight feet. Meanwhile, an iron lantern was assembled in Boston and a fine, first-order Fresnel lens shipped from Paris. By the evening of September 1, 1905, all the parts were in place, and the Graves Light flashed its first powerful beam, warning ships away from the dangerous rocks on which it stood. Now automated, the light still guides mariners with a double flash every twelve seconds.

On a dark and viciously cold morning in January 1941, the schooner *Mary O'Hara* passed Graves Ledge safely and headed for Boston's inner harbor. But the *O'Hara* would never reach the Boston wharves to deliver its load of fish. The schooner rammed an anchored barge and sank in forty feet of water, forcing the twenty-four members of its crew into the icy rigging. Their limbs freezing, the men called out for help, but no one could hear or see them. One by one, they dropped into the ocean and drowned. Only five remained when the trawler *North Star* arrived just after dawn to rescue the survivors.

Some think Graves Ledge received its rather ominous name because of tragedies such as the one that befell the *O'Hara* and its crew. Not so. The ledge is named for Thomas Graves, a prominent, early colonial Massachusetts sea trader.

The lighthouse is closed to the public and is best seen from the water. For information on tours of Boston Harbor, call (617) 536–4100.

BOSTON LIGHT
Boston Harbor, Massachusetts - 1716

A sheet of paper posted on the wall of the Boston Lighthouse contains a long and extraordinary list of names. The first name on the list is that of George Worthylake, whose tragic story is told in the introduction of this book. Then come the names of the other sixty men who have served as keepers of America's oldest and most storied light station. Consider this: The Boston Light has had half again as many keepers as the United States has had presidents. Like Worthylake, who lasted three years, some keepers stayed only a short time at the light. But others, such as Robert Ball, who kept the light from 1733 to 1774, held the job for decades, much longer than any president held office.

The Boston Light is much older than the nation it now serves. Built in 1716 by the colony of Massachusetts, it was the first true lighthouse, with tower and glassed-in lantern, in North America. To defray the expense of maintaining the light, colonial officials imposed a duty of one penny per ton on ships moving in and out of Boston Harbor. Early keepers, including Worthylake, 1716–18, and John Hayes, 1718–33, received a salary of fifty to seventy British pounds per year, which they supplemented by serving as harbor pilots.

In 1719 Hayes asked "that a great Gun be placed on the Said Island to answer Ships in a Fogg." Colonial officials liked the suggestion and brought a cannon to the island. No doubt to his chagrin, Hayes received no additional pay for firing the gun whenever fog socked in the harbor. The old cannon has survived the centuries and is now on display at the U.S. Coast Guard Academy in New London, Connecticut.

Hayes almost lost three years' salary in 1720 when a lamp overturned in the

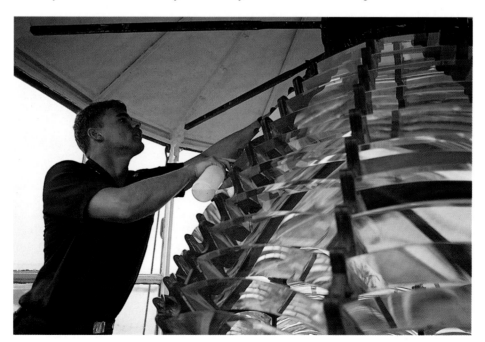

Dennis Dever, one of Americs's last lighthouse keepers, keeps the 130-year-old, second-order Fresnel lens sparkling using ordinary window cleaner. The brass frame and prisms were crafted in Paris.

A pane in the kitchen window of the keeper's house frames the oldest lighthouse in America. The building on the left houses a freshwater reservoir.

lantern, causing serious fire damage to the tower. Assuring his superiors that "ye said fire was not occasioned by ye least neglect of ye Memorialist," Hayes managed to beat back an attempt to make him pay the 216 pounds needed for repairs.

The violence of the American Revolution left only ruins on Little Brewster Island, and in 1783 the Massachusetts legislature raised 1,450 pounds to rebuild the lighthouse. For their money, the people of Massachusetts got a solid structure with walls seventy-five feet high and more than seven feet thick at the base. The tower has stood for more than 200 years, through countless gales, half a dozen hurricanes, and an assortment of fires and other calamities, all without substantial repair.

To make the light more effective, the Lighthouse Board had fourteen feet added to the height of the tower in 1859. The second-order Fresnel lens installed that same year is still in use. Today it focuses a 1,800,000-candlepower light, visible for up to sixteen miles. In inclement weather, the keepers of Boston Light continued to fire their fog cannon right up until 1850, when it was replaced by an enormous bell. Later, the station employed the strongest available trumpets, sirens, and horns to warn ships.

Despite the great power of the station's light and the strength of its fog signals, a number of ships have been lost practically within shouting distance of the lighthouse. In December 1839 three hurricanes struck Boston Harbor in less than two weeks, driving scores of vessels, including the schooner *Charlotte* and the bark *Lloyd,* onto rocks near the light. In 1861 the 991-ton square-rigger *Maritana* got caught in a blinding snowstorm in Massachusetts Bay and slammed into Shag Rocks a short distance from Boston Light. Dozens drowned or were crushed to death when the big wooden ship broke in half. Using a small dory, lighthouse personnel rescued twelve survivors who had floated to Shag Rocks on fragments of the ship. In 1882 the Shag Rocks also claimed the *Fanny Pike,* but the keeper managed to rescue the entire crew. The schooner *Calvin F. Baker* hit rocks and sank near the lighthouse during a storm in 1898. Before help could arrive, three crewmen froze to death in the rigging. On Christmas Day, 1909, the coal schooner *Davis Palmer* slammed into Finn's Ledge and went down with all hands. It is said that Captain Leroy Kowen's wife had Christmas dinner on the stove when a friend arrived with the awful news. Fate was kinder to the crew of the USS *Alacrity,* a Navy ship that hit rocks just off Little Brewster Island on February 3, 1918. The *Alacrity* sank, but its twenty-four half-frozen crewmen were rescued by keeper Charles Jennings, who had to push his dory over ice and through freezing surf to reach the wreck.

According to legend, none of the station's fog signals has ever effectively penetrated the mysterious area known as the "Ghost Walk," several miles east of the lighthouse. For reasons that are still not thoroughly understood, sailors caught in the Ghost Walk cannot hear the signal. A team of students from the Massachusetts Institute of Technology lived on Little Brewster Island for the entire summer of 1893 trying out one experimental foghorn after another. All of them failed to reach the Ghost Walk.

America's most famous lighthouse cannot be reached by land. Boston Harbor tour boats often pass by Little Brewster Island, however, and offer an excellent view of the light. For information call the Greater Boston area Visitor's Center at (617) 536–4100.

MINOTS LEDGE LIGHT
Cohasset, Massachusetts - 1850

Few navigational obstacles have destroyed as many ships and lives as Minots Ledge, a narrow, barely visible outcropping of rock just off Cohasset, Massachusetts. A survey compiled in 1847 by lighthouse inspector I. W. P. Lewis listed dozens of barks, brigs, coasters, ketches, schooners, and large ships torn apart by the ledge. At least forty lives had been snuffed out in these wrecks, and Lewis estimated property damage of more than $360,000.

Although government officials had long recognized the dangers of the ledge, none had ever seriously suggested building a lighthouse there. The feat was thought to be impossible. Any lighthouse on Minots Ledge would be exposed to the full force of the ocean. How long would it stand in a winter gale?

But Lewis was convinced that something had to be done, and armed with his survey, he forced the hand of Treasury Department Fifth Auditor Stephen Pleasonton, the country's top lighthouse official. A tightfisted conservative, Pleasonton was highly suspicious of new ideas, especially if they cost money. But in

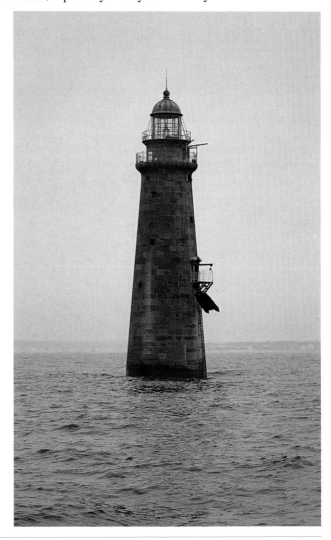

this case, Pleasonton decided to take a chance and approved plans for a radical new lighthouse design, one that showed promise of surviving the punishments of Minots Ledge.

Instead of the usual solid cylinder, the tower would consist of nine iron pilings, each of them sunk five feet into the rock and cemented in place. The keeper's dwelling and lantern would perch atop the legs, some seventy-five feet above the ravaging ocean. In theory, the tower's reinforced legs would offer little resistance to the wind and water, and even the most formidable ocean waves would pass right through the open superstructure.

The U.S. Topographical Department itself designed and built the skeleton lighthouse, for this was no

Seeming totally at the mercy of the sea, Minots Ledge Lighthouse still has a firm grip on the submerged rocks beneath it after more than 130 years. Interlocking granite blocks, some weighing two tons, help it resist giant waves.

small feat of engineering and construction. Crews worked from a schooner anchored beside the ledge, and more than once the ocean swept drill rigs and other equipment off the rocks. The work took three years and a great deal of money to complete, with a grimacing Pleasonton signing the checks. Finally, on New Year's Day in 1850, the lamps at the top of the spidery lighthouse were lit.

Captain William Smith, who designed and supervised construction of the lighthouse, proclaimed that it could weather "any storm without danger." But Isaac Dunham, the station's first keeper, did not share his confidence. Dunham, who could feel the new lighthouse swaying in the wind and hear its legs groan under the stress of constant pounding by waves, had grave doubts about the safety of the structure. Following a series of particularly violent autumn storms that "would have frightened Daniel Webster," Dunham quit the post. Dunham's resignation, after just nine months as keeper, may well have saved his life. A few months after Dunham got his feet back on solid ground, a monumental gale bowled over the lighthouse, carrying two assistant keepers to their deaths (see Introduction).

The tragedy had an unexpected casualty: It may very well have focused attention of congressmen on Pleasonton's spotty, thirty-year record as administrator of the Lighthouse Service. A congressional panel, convened during the spring of 1851, at about the time of the Minots Ledge disaster, found the nation's navigational aids in terrible shape. Pleasonton had allowed so little money to trickle through to the service that lighthouse walls were cracking and towers literally toppling into the sea. The panel learned that Pleasonton had ignored the highly effective French-made Fresnel lenses in favor of the outdated reflectors designed by his friend, Winslow Lewis. (Interestingly, Winslow Lewis was the uncle of lighthouse inspector I. W. P. Lewis, mentioned earlier.) No suggestion was made that Pleasonton had any pecuniary interest in ordering the service to use Lewis reflectors, and no such charge has ever been proven. But Congress took a dim view of the decision. Ultimately, Congress took administration of the service away from Pleasonton and placed it in the hands of a new Lighthouse Board consisting largely of engineers and mariners.

As one of its first tasks, the board undertook reconstruction of the Minots Ledge Lighthouse. The effort consumed eight years and more than $330,000, but by August 1860, the new tower was complete. This time the tower was built with granite blocks laid in parallel courses atop foundation stones weighing two tons each. In this case, at least, stone has proven stronger than iron; the lighthouse still stands, 130 years after its construction. Giant waves have actually swept over the top of the ninety-seven-foot tower, breaking windows but causing no serious structural damage.

The lantern delivers a distinctive warning to mariners: one white flash, followed by four flashes, followed by three more. The one-four-three rhythm reminds lovers of the words *I love you,* and Minots Ledge is known to the more romantically inclined as the "I Love You" light.

The lighthouse is closed to the public and cannot be reached by land. It can, however, be seen from several points along the coast near Cohasset. Boaters headed north or south along the Massachusetts coast have an excellent view of the light.

CAPE COD LIGHTS
Cape Cod, Massachusetts - 1798, 1816, 1827, 1828, 1838

Like a whirlpool of sand in the ocean, Cape Cod sweeps seaward from the far southeast corner of Massachusetts, arching to the north and finally curling back on itself about twenty miles due east of Plymouth. Deposited by glaciers that blanketed New England during much of the last 100,000 years, the sands of the cape are constantly on the move, wearing away in one area and building up in another. Land has only a tenuous hold on this place; the ocean seems always poised to rush in and reclaim the cape as its own.

But to mariners sailing westward out of the broad Atlantic, the high dunes of Cape Cod have always been a substantial and welcome sight. The Pilgrims first landed here in 1620 before sailing across Cape Cod Bay to step off onto Plymouth Rock. Once they had spotted the cape, the captains of clipper ships headed back from Europe, Africa, or China knew Boston Harbor waited less than half a day's sail to the west. A sizable number of rugged New England whalers once called the cape home, just as many fishermen do today.

But, if the cape is a friend of sailors, it is also a threat. As a point of land extending far out into the Atlantic, the cape is a formidable navigational obstacle that has ruined many good ships and killed many strong men. Four centuries of wrecks have filled the sands of its beaches with bits and pieces of vessels now long forgotten.

Cape Cod is just the sort of place where you would expect to find lighthouses, and indeed, it boasts several major lights. Most prominent is the Cape Cod Light, also known as Highland Light. The tower stands on a high bluff near Truro, and its beacon, situated 183 feet above the sea, can be seen for up to twenty-three miles. For sailors emerging from the dark reaches of the Atlantic, Cape Cod Light is often the first visual evidence that the North American continent is near.

A bank of clouds sweeps toward Highland (Cape Cod) Light from the sea.

Soon after the first Cape Cod tower was built in 1798, sailors began to confuse the light with the fixed beacon of the Boston Light forty-one miles to the northwest. To solve this problem, a rotating opaque screen was placed in the lantern. Completing one revolution every eight minutes, the screen was supposed to make the light flash. But, as one grumbling mariner was quick to point out, the screen partially obscured the light much of the time and gave it "phases, like [those of] the moon." Said he: "There are circumstances enough, at sea, to obscure the best of lights without any contrivances on shore to assist this misfortune." Objections notwithstanding, the screen system was retained for many years.

The Lighthouse Board rebuilt the old Cape Cod tower in 1857, fitting it with a first-order Fresnel lens. Rotating on a reservoir of mercury, the bull's-eye lens concentrated light into flashes of nearly 200,000 candlepower. When the station's oil lamps were replaced by a 1,000-watt electric bulb in 1932, the strength of the flash was increased to an incredible 4,000,000 candlepower. The Cape Cod Light remains one of the most powerful in America, although today it employs a dual electric beacon similar to those used at airports.

Henry David Thoreau made several visits to the Cape Cod Lighthouse during the mid-1800s. Noting rapid erosion of the sandy cliff beneath the tower, Thoreau wondered how long the lighthouse could remain on its precarious perch. Today, the edge of the cliff is only thirty feet from the base of the tower. Many believe that unless it is moved, the lighthouse will soon topple over into the Atlantic.

Hundreds of ships have ended their days on Race Point, which forms Cape Cod's westward knuckle. Vessels must round the point to reach Provincetown Harbor a few miles to the southeast, and over the years, more than a few tried but failed. No one knows exactly how many ships have piled up on the sands of the point, but more than a hundred wrecks have been noted there since the establishment of the Race Point Light in 1816. No doubt, countless others have been saved by the light's flashing white beacon, which can be seen from a distance of twelve miles.

Established in 1827 near the end of a sandy spit where the cape nearly completes a 360-degree inward spiral, Long Point Light still serves Provincetown Harbor with its flashing green light. During the Civil War, authorities responded quickly to rumors of an impending attack by Confederate warships, building a pair of small earthen gun batteries near the lighthouse on Long Point. The tiny Confederate Navy was never really up to such an expedition, however, and citizens of Provincetown soon dubbed the two batteries "Fort Harmless" and "Fort Useless."

The Nauset Beach Light, first lighted in 1838, guards Cape Cod's Atlantic coast south of the Cape Cod Light. Originally, the Nauset station displayed three lights shining from identical towers known to many locals as the "Three Sisters of Nauset." Eventually, the government determined that one light would

Looking like a rock on a chessboard, Long Point Lighthouse marks the end of a sandy arm of land curving back toward Provincetown on Cape Cod. The panels outside the lantern convert sunlight to electricity to power the lamp.

serve just as well as three, whereupon two of Nauset's maidens suffered the indignity of being sold and converted for use as summer cottages. A new tower was erected in 1923 and guides ships with alternating red and white flashes.

In Woods Hole at the cape's far southwestern tip, the Nobska Light warns ships away from a pair of vicious shoals called the Hedge Fence and L'Hommedieu. The first lighthouse here, built in 1828, was a simple stone cottage

with a lantern on top, but in 1876, the Lighthouse Board approved a new tower for the Nobska station. An iron shell was built in Chelsea, Massachusetts, and shipped to the cape in four sections. Work crews at Nobska erected the shell and lined it with brick. The tower stands forty-two feet above the ground and eighty-seven feet above the sea. Its fourth-order Fresnel lens throws out a 28,000-candle-power light visible from sixteen miles at sea. The light flashes once every six seconds. Sailors nearing the shoals see a red light while those in safe water see a white light.

Nauset Beach Lighthouse looks toward the sea with its big red eye.

For Highland Light: *From U.S. 6 in Truro take Highland Avenue and follow signs to the light. The lighthouse is not open to the public. Because of severe erosion, there is no access to the beach here.*

For Race Point Light: *From U.S. 6 in Provincetown take Race Point Road to Race Point Beach. A visit to this lighthouse is recommended only for veteran walkers. Two miles of soft sand separate the parking area from the light. The National Park Service closes this area to protect thousands of nesting terns during mating season, but they might just as well leave the area open; the terns have their own very effective means of keeping you at a distance. If you would prefer to avoid the long walk and the hostility of the terns, then substitute a visit to the informative Life Saving Museum near the beach.*

For Long Point Light: *Take a short boat ride across the harbor from Provincetown. Rental boats and regular shuttles are available in Provincetown during the summer.*

For Nauset Beach Light: *From U.S. 6 take Brackett Road and follow the signs to Nauset Light Beach. The light is closed to the public but can be seen from the National Seashore parking area. However, the original "Three Sisters," long out of service, have been reunited and can be visited with a short walk down a paved trail from the Nauset Light Beach parking lot.*

The four lighthouses listed above are all located within the Cape Cod National Seashore. Unauthorized vehicle and foot traffic contributes to the erosion that is eating up parts of the cape. Please enjoy, but do not destroy, this treasure. For more information about Cape Cod, call the National Seashore Headquarters at (508) 349–3785.

For Nobska Light: *From Falmouth follow Woods Hole Road for three miles until it becomes Main Street in the village of Woods Hole. Turn left on Church Street, which will take you to one of the most picturesque lighthouses in all of New England.*

NANTUCKET LIGHTS

Brant Point and Great Point on Nantucket Island, Massachusetts
1746 and 1784

Nothing is more democratic than a New England town meeting. If a town is to part with so much as a dime, then a majority of the community must agree to spending it. And since no one wants to appear loose with their neighbors' money, the budgets that emerge from town meetings are notoriously tightfisted. So it is surprising that America's second-oldest light station owes its existence to a town meeting held on Nantucket Island on January 24, 1746. On that day the sea captains of the island addressed their fellow citizens and asked for a lighthouse to help them find the harbor. In a rare fit of fiscal openhandedness, the people of Nantucket offered to raise 200 English pounds for the project, and not long after, a little wooden lighthouse was built on Brant Point at the entrance to Nantucket Harbor. At the time, only one other lighthouse stood in all of North America: the stone-towered Boston Light on Little Brewster Island.

Unfortunately, the Brant Point Light would not have as distinguished a career as its big neighbor to the north. It burned to the ground only a dozen years after its

construction. At another town meeting the following year, citizens once again opened their purses, and money was raised for a second tower. This one was knocked down by a windstorm in 1774. The *Massachusetts Gazette* reported: "We hear from Nantucket that on Wednesday the 9th of March, Instant at about 8 o'clock, they had a most violent Gust of Wind that perhaps was ever known there, but it lasted only a minute. It seemed to come in a narrow Vein, and in its progress blew down and totally destroyed the Light-House on that Island besides several Shops, Barns, etc."

The citizens of Nantucket then paid for yet another tower, which burned down in 1783. At this point, the islanders may have felt they were throwing good money after bad, and the next light erected on Brant Point was nothing more than a lantern hoisted on a pole. Its light was so dim that sailors compared it to the glow of a lightning bug. Eventually, this unsatisfactory "bug light" was abandoned. Subsequent lights on the point were destroyed by storms,

As many as ten houses have stood on Nantucket's Brant Point since islanders built the first one here in 1746. This small tower has stood since 1901. (Courtesy U.S. Coast Guard)

ruined by rot and salt water, condemned by inspectors, pulled down by the Lighthouse Board, and otherwise undone so that, in all, a total of ten lighthouses have stood there.

Perhaps surprisingly, the current lighthouse has survived since 1901. Its white cylindrical wooden tower raises its lantern only twenty-six feet above the water, making it the lowest light in New England. Focused by a fourth-order Fresnel lens, its red light can be seen from about ten miles away.

The Great Point Light on the opposite side of the island has been less exasperating for the local citizenry. Built in 1784, it burned down only once, in 1816. Better still, from the point of view of the islanders, the original tower was paid for by the Commonwealth of Massachusetts, and its replacement, completed in 1816, by the U.S. government. Built of stone, the 1816 tower stood just over seventy feet tall. It displayed a fixed white light visible from about fourteen miles at sea. Sailors approaching the dangerous Cross Rip or Tuckernuck shoals saw a red light.

The charming island of Nantucket can be reached by auto ferry from New Bedford, Falmouth, and Hyannis Port. In most cases reservations are required. For ferry information and reservations call Hi-Line Cruise in Hyannis Port at (508) 775–7185 or the Massachusetts Steamship Authority in Falmouth at (508) 548–3788. The ferries provide an excellent view of both lighthouses.

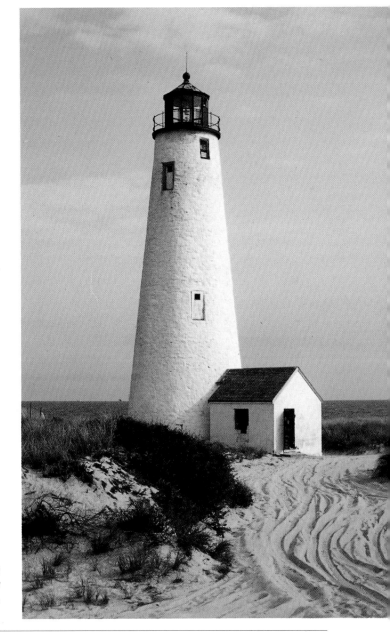

Nantucket's Great Point Lighthouse looked like this during the 1970s. This tower was knocked down by a storm and has recently been replaced by another, similar in appearance. (Courtesy U.S. Coast Guard)

GAY HEAD LIGHT

Martha's Vineyard, Massachusetts - 1799

Of the several lighthouses on Martha's Vineyard, the oldest and best known is the Gay Head Light. The headland takes its name from the bright colors streaking its cliffs. The tower built atop the cliffs in 1799 took advantage of their considerable height to raise its lantern 160 feet above the sea. To manage this lofty light station, the government hired a man with the unlikely name of Ebenezer Skiff. As it turned out, Skiff had a gift for gab, and at least twice during his career at Gay Head, he managed to talk his superiors into granting him a substantial raise. Few lighthouse keepers in that era ever accomplished such a feat.

The original Gay Head lighthouse had an eight-sided wooden tower rising fifty-one feet above the cliff tops on a stone foundation. The Lighthouse Board ordered construction of a new tower in 1856, and this time the builder used brick. A first-order Fresnel lens focused the light, which could be seen from a distance of nineteen miles. The huge first-order lens has been replaced, but the light still throws out its distinct combination of three white flashes and one red flash every forty seconds.

Martha's Vineyard also boasts lighthouses at East Chop, West Chop, Edgartown, and Cape Poge, located on the northeastern point of Chappaquidick Island. When eroding cliffs threatened the Cape Poge Light in 1987, it was lifted by a sky crane and moved back some 500 feet.

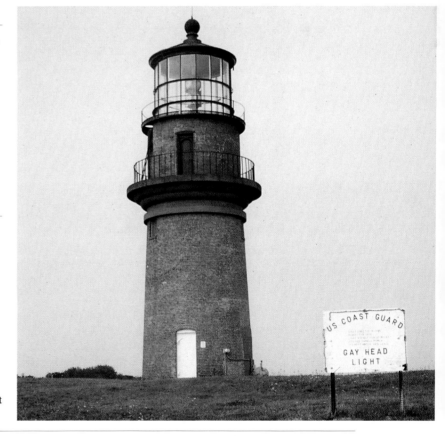

During the summer, the delightful island of Martha's Vineyard can be reached by auto ferry from several points in southern Massachusetts. For departures from New Bedford call (508) 997–1688; from Falmouth call (508) 548–3788; and from Hyannis Port call (508) 775–7185. The Gay Head lighthouse is about fifteen miles west of Edgartown or the Vineyard Haven ferry slips and can be reached by a paved road.

Built atop a high cliff, Gay Head Lighthouse on Martha's Vineyard throws its light seaward from a point 160 feet above the water. (Courtesy U.S. Coast Guard)

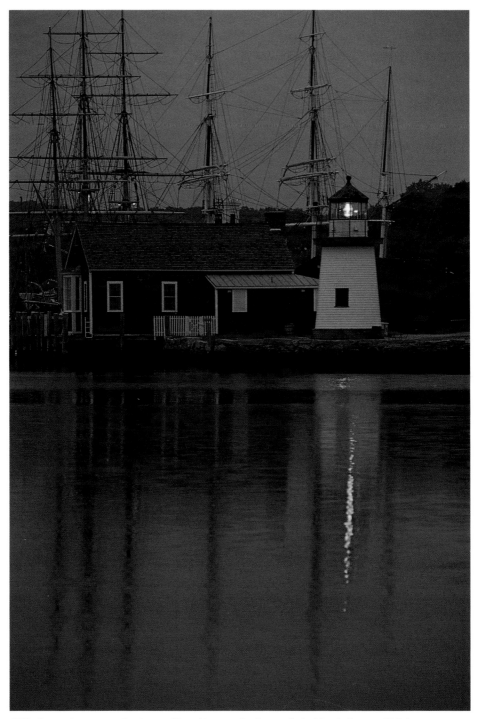

With the soaring masts of antique sailing ships as a background, the Mystic Seaport Lighthouse coaxes visitors back into the eighteenth and nineteenth centuries. The lighthouse is a copy of the one at Brant Point on Nantucket.

CHAPTER FOUR

LIGHTS OF
THE LIBERTY LADIES

Rhode Island, Connecticut, New York and New Jersey

Lights of the Liberty Ladies

New York City

Sandy Hook

Navesink
Highlands

Trenton

Atlantic Ocean

NEW JERSEY

Barnegat

LONG BEACH ISLAND

Cape May

HARPER'S WEEKLY.

A JOURNAL OF CIVILIZATION

VOL. XIII.—No. 657.] NEW YORK, SATURDAY, JULY 31, 1869. [SINGLE COPIES, TEN CENTS.
[$4.00 PER YEAR IN ADVANCE.

Entered according to Act of Congress, in the Year 1869, by Harper & Brothers, in the Clerk's Office of the District Court of the United States, for the Southern District of New York.

The only lighthouse keeper to appear on the cover of Harper's Weekly, *the* Life Magazine *of its day, was Ida Lewis. Her rescues in Newport Harbor won her national acclaim and dozens of marriage proposals.*

When Ulysses S. Grant stepped out of his freshly painted presidential launch one summer day in 1869, he missed Lime Rock altogether and ended up standing ankle deep in Newport Harbor. The scene is easy to imagine: horrified aides and stout young sailors in immaculate uniforms piling over the side of the boat and splashing through the shallow water to the president's side and the old, bearded soldier waving them all back with his cane. Grant had gotten his feet wet plenty of times before—in the trenches at Richmond and Petersburg—and saw no reason now to let a little harmless sea water stop him short of his objective.

"I have come to see Ida Lewis," said the president. "To see her I'd get wet up to my armpits."

President Grant was certainly neither the first nor the last man to ruin his shoes in order to see a lady. But he was probably the first U.S. president to do so while on his way to visit a lady lighthouse keeper.

Miss Lewis graciously received Grant and just as graciously ignored his squishing shoes. She took his arm and led him on a tour of her tiny island, only a few times larger in area than the lighthouse itself. She showed him the workings of the light. She told him about life on Lime Rock, and he, perhaps, told her about his campaigns in the South. Their chat was warm, friendly, almost matter-of-fact. And why not? It was only natural the two should meet. Having just moved into the White House and still basking in the popular glow of his victories over the Confederates in Virginia, Grant was the best-known man in America. And Ida Lewis was her country's most famous woman.

THE LADY OF LIME ROCK

At the time of Grant's visit in 1869, Ida Lewis was twenty-seven years old. She had already lived on Lime Rock for a dozen years and saved the lives of several people. Sketches of her attractive face and trim figure had appeared in magazines and newspapers all over the country, along with sensational stories about her rescues and other exploits. She had become a national heroine, a kind of nineteenth-century starlet, and all without ever leaving Newport or traveling more than a mile or two from her rock.

When she was born in 1842, her parents weighed her down with the name Idawalley Zorada, but she would bear this burden, along with many others, handily in a life that lasted only one season less than seven decades. Her father was Captain Hosea Lewis, a Revenue-Cutter pilot who was retired to the supposedly more sedentary Lighthouse Service because of ill health. While Ida was still in her early teens, Captain Lewis became so sick that she and her mother were forced to take over running the Lime Rock Light. In addition to her duties at the lighthouse, Ida also rowed her younger sisters and brother back and forth to school each day. She made her daily trip to Newport regardless of gales or blizzards, and on more than one occasion, when she returned to her home on the rock, she was forced to cut her frozen stockings off her legs with a knife.

Sometimes storms caught Ida and the other Lewis children in the harbor in their open boat. Watching Ida pull against the waves with the oars, Captain Lewis felt especially helpless. "I have watched until I could bear it no longer," he said, "expecting every moment to see them swamped and the crew at the mercy of the waves. . . . Old sailor that I am . . . I could not endure to see them perish and realize that [I was] powerless to save them." But as the old seaman would eventually realize, his children were as safe with Ida as they would have been with anyone.

In the fall of 1858, at the age of sixteen, Ida glanced out the window of the lighthouse and saw an overturned sailboat and four young men desperately flailing at the cold harbor water. In a blink she had the station lifeboat out of the boathouse and was cutting smartly toward the scene of the accident. When she reached the drowning boys, she maneuvered carefully to approach them one at a time. Otherwise, in their panic, they might have overturned her boat, with unfortunate results for all concerned. As it was, she managed to pull all four aboard and row them safely to land. As any boys might have been, the four were deeply ashamed of having been rescued by a girl. They were not anxious to talk about the incident afterward, and the story of their rescue by young Ida Lewis was not widely known until many years later. Weeden King, one of the young men she rescued, later became Lieutenant King of the Union Army. Three years after surviving the near disaster in Newport Harbor, King lost his life in the much more tragic calamity of Bull Run.

The end of the Civil War left the troops at Newport's Fort Adams with little to do, and like bored soldiers everywhere, they often found relief at the bottom of a bottle. One day in February 1866, three drunken warriors were returning to the fort from Newport where they had celebrated, no doubt for the 100th time, the victory of the Union. Spying a skiff, which, as it happened, belonged to the Lewis family, the three decided to take a shortcut across the harbor to the fort. One of the soldiers sang while his buddies pulled at the oars, and stomping in time with his sour notes, put his foot right through the bottom of the boat. The oarsmen managed to swim to shore, but the tipsy singer would have drowned had not the arms of a strong young woman looped a stout rope under his armpits. Unable to lift the man into her boat, Ida Lewis towed him to shore. There she left him to face the ire of his officers and the inevitable torments of a Civil War-size hangover.

One year later, three negligent laborers allowed a prized sheep belonging to their employer to run off toward the harbor. Before they could catch the woolly creature, it fell into the harbor and was swept by the tide out toward Narragansett Bay. Fearing for their jobs, the men jumped into the keeper's skiff and pulled hard for the foundering sheep. But none of the three was an experienced waterman; a wave rolled them over, and they found themselves treading water along with the sheep. Again, Ida Lewis came to the rescue of men who had stolen a boat belonging to her own family. When she got the men ashore, she turned back toward the bay and saved the unfortunate sheep as well.

Ida Lewis effected several more dramatic rescues, but the one that earned her nationwide fame took place in a winter gale on March 29, 1869. She was sick with a severe cold at the time and had huddled beside the kitchen stove much of the day with her shoes off and a blanket thrown over her shoulders. Late in the day her mother cried out to her. The big waves churned up by the storm had thrown over a boat in the harbor, and men were drowning. Although her mother tried to stop her, Ida ran for the lifeboat. With no shoes and her stockinged feet immersed in freezing water, she fought off one big wave after another. If she had reached the capsized boat only a few moments later, the two numb and exhausted soldiers struggling nearby would have slipped under the water. Ida pulled them aboard, but this rescue would not be a complete success. Although she rowed in circles and called out, the boy who had piloted the soldiers' boat did not answer. He was gone forever.

The story of this exploit reached the pages of most of the major newspapers in the country. Engraved pictures of Ida and her Lime Rock Lighthouse were published in *Leslie's* magazine and in *Harper's Weekly*. Suddenly, she started receiving barrels of mail and visits from the rich, powerful, and famous. The Astors, Belmonts, and Vanderbilts all made social calls at the rock as did President Grant, Vice President Schuyler Colfax, and William Tecumseh Sherman. People gave her boats, medals, and gifts of money. She got offers from agents who wanted to put her on the stage. But she remained on Lime Rock with her family and her lighthouse.

Sandwiched into the stacks of mail that ended up on the lighthouse kitchen table day after day were more than a few marriage proposals. Men from every corner of the country sent her trinkets and dried flowers and asked for her hand. But the only proposal she ever accepted was that of William Wilson, a sometime fisherman and yacht captain who once moored his vessel near the rock. Their marriage was unhappy, however, and the restless sailor soon put to sea. Although she never saw Wilson again, she had only one answer to those who suggested she divorce him: "Whom God has joined together let no man put asunder."

Perhaps Wilson is not altogether to blame for the failure of his marriage to

The Keeper of Execution Rocks Lighthouse makes an urgent call on a radio telephone during the 1940s.

Execution Rocks got its name during the Revolutionary War when the British were said to have chained prisoners here and allowed them to drown at high tide. This photograph dates from the late 1940s.

Ida. Maybe he felt she could never really be his wife since she was already married to the Lime Rock Lighthouse. Like her legal marriage to Wilson, the latter union lasted until her death in 1911. When her father died in 1872, she was officially appointed assistant keeper, and after her mother's death seven years later, she became keeper. In all, she tended the light for more than half a century. When the sad news came on October 24, 1911, that Ida Lewis had died, the bells of vessels in Newport Harbor tolled through the night.

OTHER LADIES

Ida Lewis was only one of thousands of women who found it their calling in life to turn lighthouses into lighthomes. Some were married to keepers or were the helpful daughters of lighthousemen. Others were keepers themselves. Whatever their titles or status, these tough women endured the same cold, isolation, and poverty as the men who tended lights. Without them our country could not have grown and prospered as it did. Without them many of the millions of immigrants who sought the promise of America might never have reached these shores safely.

For most immigrants, the first glimpse of America was the flash of a lighthouse beacon. And for many, the most memorable sight on their first day in the United States was a structure not widely known as a lighthouse—but a lighthouse it was, nonetheless. The Statue of Liberty, the First Lady of the Hudson herself, was once a navigational light. Given to America by France at roughly the time Ida Lewis became keeper at Lime Rock, the statue, then called *Liberty Enlightening the World,* was lighted and began guiding ships in 1886. Not surprisingly, the flame of the Lady's torch was used as the lantern. The torch has been dark, coincidentally, since about the time Ida Lewis died. But the enduring humanitarian spirit symbolized by these ladies, each in her own way, still burns brightly. So long as their spirit lives, we need not fear the lights will go out.

A popular resort during the late 1900s, Block Island still attracts many visitors. Shown here at dusk, the island community retains the charm of a bygone era.

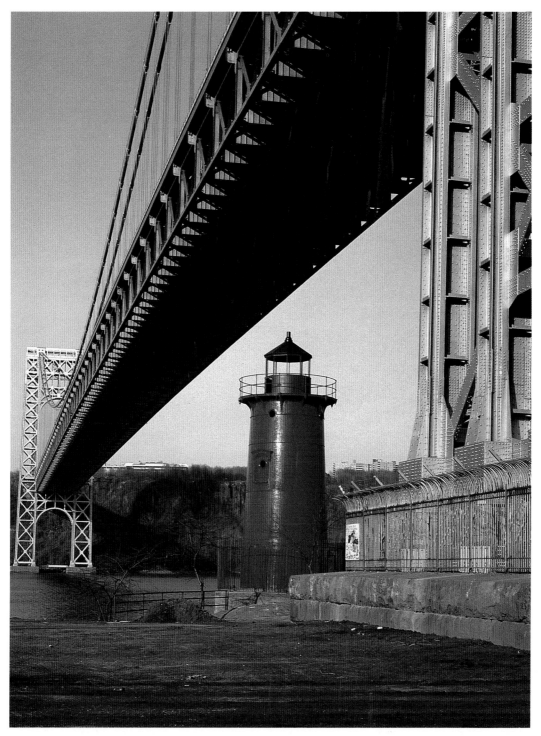

*George Washington Bridge dwarfs tiny **Jeffrey's Hook Lighthouse** on New York City's Hudson shore. When the giant bridge was completed in 1931, the lighthouse was no longer needed. Much to the delight of children, who know it as the "Little Red Lighthouse," the colorful tower survives today as a much-loved attraction of Fort Washington Park.* (© William Kaufhold)

BEAVERTAIL LIGHT
Conanicut Island, Rhode Island - 1749

America's third lighthouse, after the Boston and Brant Point lights, was built at Beavertail Point on Conanicut Island south of Jamestown in 1749. Officials of the Rhode Island colony felt the light was needed to guide ships around the point and into Newport Harbor or Narragansett Bay.

Conanicut Island was already famous for its association with Captain William Kidd, known to some as a privateer and to the people he robbed as a pirate. During the late 1600s Captain Kidd frequented the island, using it as a kind of hideout. Some say he buried a substantial treasure here. If the treasure exists, it has never been found, but Kidd himself was found. Lured to Boston by Governor Bellomont, a former friend, Kidd was captured and eventually hanged in London.

During the Revolutionary War, the British treated Beavertail Light almost as roughly as they had dealt with Captain Kidd many years before. In the summer of 1775 the British sailed into Newport Harbor and, when they left four years later, burned the Beavertail Lighthouse. The rubblestone tower survived the burning, but it was not fully repaired and back in operation until 1790.

The present square granite tower was built in 1856. Its fourth-order Fresnel lens flashes a green light eight times each minute from a height of sixty-four feet above the sea.

During the mid-1800s, the station had a one-horsepower fog signal. Whenever fog or heavy weather set in, the keeper walked his trusty old nag on a treadmill, operating a pump that provided pressure for the horn.

From the east side of the Newport Bridge on Route 138 take East Shore Road through Jamestown and follow signs to Beavertail State Park. This historic lighthouse is a "must visit," especially for those who enjoy watching ocean waves crash against rocks.

In Rhode Island it is possible to visit or at least see several lighthouses in one day. The square-towered Dutch Island Light, a Narragansett Bay light station established in 1826 and inactive since 1947, can be seen from a camping area south of Jamestown. Plum Beach Light, a caisson-style or spark-plug lighthouse, built in 1897 and deactivated in 1941, can be seen from the Jamestown Bridge.

The square, granite tower of Beavertail Lighthouse rises above the southern end of Rhode Island's Conanicut Island. British redcoats burned an earlier lighthouse here during the Revolutionary War.

POINT JUDITH LIGHT
Point Judith, Rhode Island - 1810

One of several dangerous coastal areas known to sailors as the "graveyard of the Atlantic," Point Judith has threatened mariners with its shoals since the first European ships arrived to explore these shores. The point, which thrusts several miles out into the Atlantic, is especially menacing in a storm. As early as the American Revolution, a beacon was maintained there to warn ships, but no lighthouse was built on the point until 1810. In that year the government hired contractor Daniel Way to construct a tower. A crude wooden structure, Way's tower was blown over by a gale in 1815.

By 1816 a second, sturdier lighthouse stood on the point. Its cylindrical walls, made of rough stone and cement, rose thirty-five feet above the ground and seventy-five feet above the sea. Driven by a clockwork mechanism powered by a 288-pound weight, the lamps and lenses rotated on a copper table so that sailors saw a flash every two and a half minutes.

The Lighthouse Board ordered construction of the present Point Judith Lighthouse in 1857. Its octagonal, granite-block tower stands sixty-five feet above the water, and its light, focused by a fourth-order Fresnel lens, has a range of sixteen miles. The light occults, or goes dark briefly, every fifteen seconds.

Despite the presence of a light on Point Judith, its shoals have continued to destroy ships. The *Normandy* (1864), *American Eagle* (1870), *Acusionet* (1870), *Venus* (1877), *Cucktoo* (1882), *Harry Barry* (1888), *Anita* (1888), *Mars* (1892), *Blue Jay* (1896), *Amanda E.* (1902), *Comet* (1973), and countless other vessels have been lost nearby.

On some early maps the area is marked as "Point Juda Neck." Perhaps that is how it got its present name. But according to an often-told, whimsical story, the point was given its name by an old, nearsighted sea captain whose daughter Judy was the first aboard his small vessel to spot the point. Unable to see the land himself, the captain cried out, "Point, Judy!"

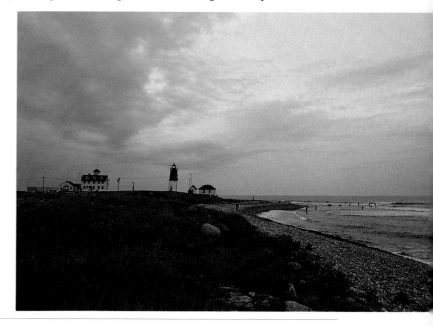

From U.S. 1 drive south on Route 108 to the Coast Guard Station at Point Judith. Strewn with rocks and pebbles polished by the surf, the beaches here are very beautiful.

Point Judith Light shines over one of the most dangerous stretches of America's Atlantic coast. Killer storms and shoals, lurking just beneath the surface, have destroyed countless ships within sight of this light.

WATCH HILL LIGHT
Watch Hill, Rhode Island - 1807

The people of Rhode Island built a watchtower on strategic Watch Hill during King George's War (1744–48). Its purpose, however, was not to guide ships but, rather, to provide early warning of a naval attack. No such attack came, and the tower fell into ruin. A gale wiped away all traces of the watchtower in 1781.

Although the importance of Watch Hill as a mark for vessels moving in and out of Block Island Sound was widely recognized, no lighthouse was built here until the early nineteenth century. In 1806 the Lighthouse Service hired Elisha Woodward of New London, Connecticut, to build a round wooden tower and protect its walls with shingles. A bank of ten whale-oil lamps provided the light.

In 1855, during the flurry of lighthouse construction started after the Lighthouse Board took charge of American navigational aids, a new tower appeared on watch Hill. Built with long, rectangular blocks of gray granite, it placed the focal plain of its light sixty-one feet above the sound.

Originally, the lantern displayed a fixed white light focused by a fourth-order Fresnel lens. But early in this century, when bright street lights began to compete with the lighthouse and confuse navigators, the lens was replaced with a rotating optic displaying a flashing white light every fifteen seconds.

Take Route 1A from Westerly to Watch Hill and park in the village. The light cannot be seen from the village, but it is just over the hill, and you can easily walk to it, although only the grounds are open to the public. The village offers several charming shops and restaurants.

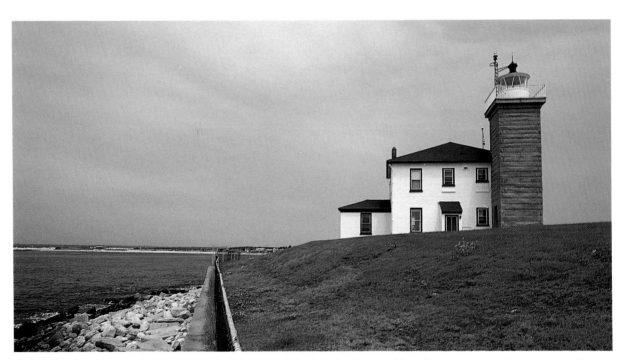

Colonial soldiers once stood on a tower nearby here to watch for the sails of enemy ships. Nowadays, sailors keep an eye out for the beacon of the Watch Hill Lighthouse.

BLOCK ISLAND LIGHTS
Block Island, Rhode Island - 1829 and 1875

Helmsmen give Block Island a wide berth. Ringed by submerged boulders and sandy shoals, the six-mile-long island has ended the careers of countless ships and no few sailors. In a single twenty-year stretch during the early 1800s, thirty-four schooners, fifteen sloops, eight brigs, and two larger ships wrecked on Block Island.

To cut these losses, the Lighthouse Service built a tower on Sandy Point, a finger of land pointing north toward Point Judith. Constructed at a cost of $15,000, the tower stood forty-five feet high; its light could be seen for twelve miles. The rapidly shifting sands of Sandy Point proved almost as liquid as the sea, however, and the lighthouse had to be rebuilt three times to pull it back from the encroaching ocean.

The present Block Island North (Sandy Point) Lighthouse, built in 1867, served for more than a century before it was deactivated and replaced in 1970 by an automated offshore beacon. Somewhat resembling a church or schoolhouse, it

For more than a century, the Block Island North Lighthouse guided sailors around a bank of deadly shoals. Renovated in 1993, the lighthouse draws many visitors.

was made of brownish-gray granite and had a brown, metal-walled lantern protruding from its roof. The lantern once housed a fourth-order Fresnel lens and cast over the water an occulting white light that could be seen from about thirteen miles away. Hiram Ball, who successfully promoted Block island as a swank, Victorian resort, also served for many years as the keeper of North Light. Ball could truthfully boast to the island's wealthy visitors that he had been appointed to the post by President Abraham Lincoln.

Ball was long gone from the North Light by February 1907, when the steamer *Larchmont* ran into the schooner *Henry Knowlton* just off the northwest coast of Block Island. The *Larchmont* got the worst of the collision and rapidly sank, dumping 150 passengers and crew into the freezing waters of Block Island Sound. Only nineteen of those aboard the *Larchmont* survived. The *Knowlton* also sank, but more slowly, and its crew rowed to safety near the Watch Hill Light several miles to the northwest.

Among the most remarkable structures in America is the Block Island Southeast Lighthouse, built high on the Mohegan Bluffs in 1875. The sixty-seven-foot, octagonal tower and attached Victorian-style keeper's duplex were constructed of red brick. Because of the considerable elevation of the bluffs, the lantern throws out its flashing green light from a point more than 200 feet above the water. The light is focused by a huge first-order Fresnel lens fashioned by the Henry Lapaute Company of Paris for $10,000; its name is found on some of the brass fittings of the lens. The entire station cost the U.S. Treasury more than

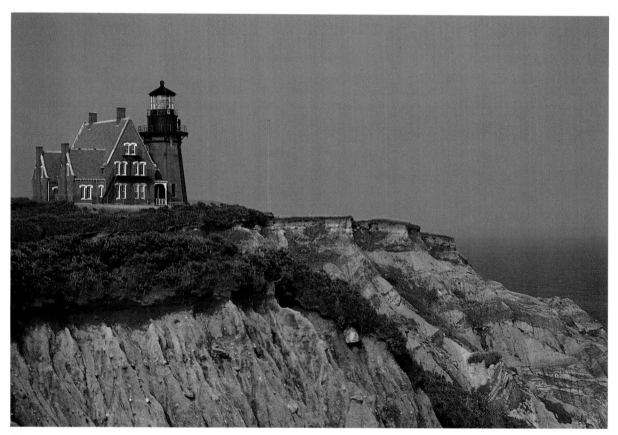

The perfect setting for a Victorian novel, Block Island Southeast Lighthouse commands a lofty, heavily eroded bluff. To keep the old lighthouse from falling into the ocean, conservationists moved it inland in 1993.

$75,000 to build, but the light's first keeper, Henry Clark, was paid only $600 a year to manage it.

Not far from the granite foundations of the lighthouse, cliffs drop sharply into the ocean more than 160 feet below. These cliffs must have seemed even loftier to the war party of fifty Mohegan Indians who were trapped here in 1590. The Mohegans, who were from Long Island, appeared suddenly in their war canoes and launched a raid against the local Indians. But the Block Island warriors quickly defeated the invaders, drove them back to the bluffs, and threw them over the cliffs.

In 1993 the 2,000-ton Block Island Southeast Lighthouse was carefully moved 300 feet back from the sea. It was through the efforts of a dedicated group of volunteers that the necessary funds were raised.

Laced with Victorian charm, Block Island is well worth the long ferry ride from New London, Connecticut, or Galilee, Rhode Island. So are its lighthouses, both of which can be reached from the ferry slip by automobile, taxi, or bicycle. The Southeast Light stands just above the village on the Mohegan Bluffs. A visit to the inactive North Light, about six miles north of the village, requires a mile-long trek through deep sand. Thousands of seagulls flock in the area and are under the impression that the place belongs to them. When disturbed, they can make more noise and commotion than you might think possible.

For ferry schedules and reservations call (203) 442–9553 in Connecticut or (401) 789–3502 in Rhode Island. For lighthouse information or to help with further restoration, contact the Block Island Southeast Foundation, P.O. Box 949, Block Island, Rhode Island 02807.

OTHER RHODE ISLAND LIGHTS
1870, 1871

Atlases will tell you that with a mere 1,214 square miles to call its own, Rhode Island is America's smallest state. But this is only a technical description. As the "Ocean State," Rhode Island lays claim to a province that stretches clear around the world. Rhode Island has always extended its hand to the sea, and for much of its history, a majority of its citizens have earned their livings through maritime enterprises. So it should come as no surprise that at one time or another, at least thirty lighthouses have shined from its shores. Few states have ever boasted so many.

Only ten of Rhode Island's lighthouses are now active. Some of the inactive towers were pulled down by the government. Others burned or were bowled over by storms. But happily, most remain, and a growing number of citizens are joining organizations dedicated to restoring and preserving the old lighthouses.

Among the most interesting of the inactive Rhode Island lighthouses is Rose Island Light near Newport. Built in 1870 on top of old Fort Hamilton, the station served for a century before the Coast Guard darkened its lantern in 1971. With a small tower rising from the roof of a stone keeper's dwelling, it guided mariners sailing the lower reaches of Narragansett Bay. Construction of the Newport Bridge, which served more effectively as a navigational marker, made the Rose Island Light obsolete. This light must have been a familiar sight to Ida Lewis, heroine and famed keeper of the Lime Rock Light in Newport Harbor.

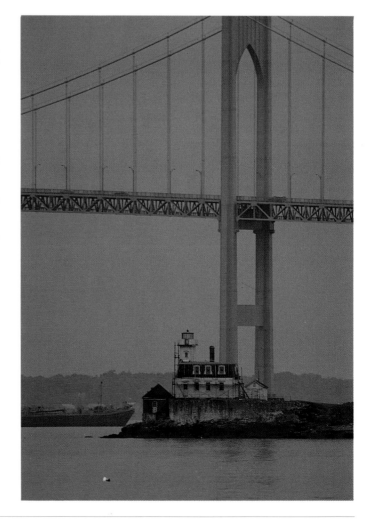

Serving as an enormous navigational marker, the Newport Bridge dwarfs the little lighthouse far below its spans. Made an anachronism by the bridge, Rose Island Light was deactivated in 1971. Today, it has been lovingly restored. The Rose Island Lighthouse operates as a museum by day and a bed and breakfast by night. For information, call the Rose Island Lighthouse office at (401) 847-4242.

Built in 1871, only one year after the Rose Island Light, the Pomham Rocks Light served until 1974. A steel tower now does the job of warning ships away from the dangerous rocks that threaten ships plying the East Providence River. The old station, now owned by the Mobil Oil Company, consists of a wooden Victorian-style house with a small tower and lantern on top.

Rose Island Light: Motorists crossing the Newport Bridge enjoy an elevated view of the lighthouse, but for a more relaxed look, visit Fort Adams State Park off Harris Avenue in Newport. While in the Newport area, watch for the green flash of the Newport Harbor Light on the northern toe of Goat Island. Also in Newport is the old Lime Rock Lighthouse. The lighthouse now serves as headquarters of the Ida Lewis Yacht Club. Members maintain the light as a memorial to Lewis. Another treat in Newport is the Castle Hill Lighthouse near the Coast Guard Station on Castle Hill Road. Built in 1890, it continues to warn sailors with a red light flashing every six seconds.

Pomham Rocks Light: Unfortunately, this interesting structure is closed to the public and is very difficult to see from any convenient vantage point in Providence. You may catch a glimpse of it from Route 103.

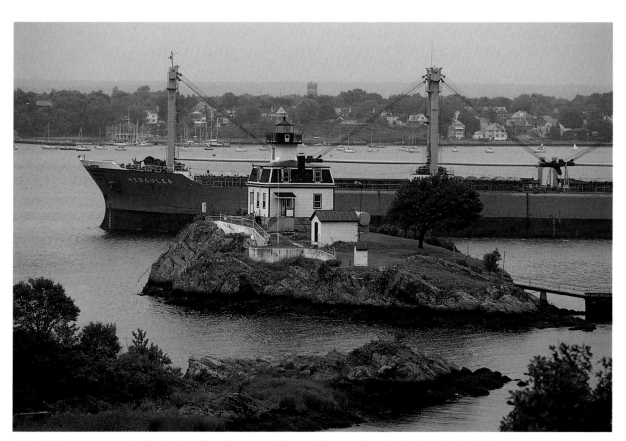

It looks like a near miss, but the freighter Hercules *is actually a safe distance from the Pomham Rocks Lighthouse.*

NEW LONDON HARBOR LIGHT
New London, Connecticut - 1760

The citizens of states in the northeast are quite familiar with lotteries. Tickets for weekly cash-prize drawings can often be purchased in gas stations, small grocery stores, and sometimes even in restaurants. Proceeds from the lotteries are usually used to pay for roads, bridges, schools, and similar projects. Colonial Americans also practiced this mild, civic-minded form of gambling. In fact, the people of New London, Connecticut, raised money for the town's first lighthouse with a lottery. No record remains of how much money the lottery raised,

The New London Lighthouse has weathered countless storms since its construction in 1769 with money raised in a lottery. (© Thomas Hahn)

108

but it was enough to build a stone tower sixty-four feet high and twenty-four feet in diameter at the base. A tonnage tax was imposed on shipping to pay the keeper and maintain the lighthouse. When the whale-oil lamps of the New London tower were first lit in 1760, only three other lighthouses marked the coasts of colonial America.

Unlike the Boston Light, the lighthouse at New London survived the Revolutionary War. In fact, American privateers used the beacon to help them find shelter from British warships. But while the light escaped the violence of our nation's first war, it did not long survive the ravages of wind and weather. By 1799 a ten-foot crack had opened in its walls, and the U.S. government decided to tear it down and rebuild. The new lighthouse, erected near the site of its predecessor, has proven far more durable. Built in 1801 for $15,547.90, the octagonal sandstone tower and separate keeper's dwelling still stand.

The tower rises ninety feet above an outcropping of rocks on the banks of the Thames River. Its lantern houses a fourth-order Fresnel lens focusing a 6,000-candlepower white light. A red sector in the light warns ships away from Sarah Ledge and other shoals to the west of the harbor.

The grounds and keeper's dwelling are privately owned and closed to the public, but the lighthouse can be seen from Pequot Avenue near Ocean Beach. Nearly two centuries old, the tower rises from a rocky outcropping on the west bank of the Thames River.

A few miles to the west of New London, just off I-95, is Mystic Seaport, an authentically restored nineteenth-century coastal village. The seaport boasts more than 300 antique vessels as well as its own lighthouse, a reproduction of the Brant Point Light on Nantucket. Although the lighthouse is not original, it does give visitors a sense of how harbor lights served seamen. With the high masts of the Charles W. Morgan and Joseph Conrad sailing ships in the background, it also provides a tempting opportunity for photographers. A fourth-order Fresnel lens is on display in the seaport visitors' center.

NEW LONDON LEDGE LIGHT

New London, Connecticut - 1909

This three-story mansion is located in a very exclusive neighborhood. There is room here for only one house. The street that runs in front of the mansion—and on all four sides—is Long Island Sound. Freighters, ferries, and pleasure craft sail by at all hours of the day and night. We must assume the designers of the New London Ledge Lighthouse had a sense of humor. Why else would they build a French Second Empire-style edifice on a submerged ledge at the entrance to New London Harbor? Perhaps no other lighthouse in America seems so out of character with its surroundings.

Built in 1909 for $93,968, a large sum at the time, the Ledge Lighthouse was supposed to do what the New London Harbor Light could not do in fog and foul weather: warn ships away from the dangerous shoals near the mouth of the Thames River. The lantern, rising from the center of the roof like a cupola, once housed a fourth-order Fresnel lens which floated on a reservoir of mercury. A clockwork mechanism rotated the lens, causing the light to flash. The old lens, produced in Paris by Henry Lapaute, has been removed and replaced by a smaller automated lens. Sailors see three white flashes and then one red flash every thirty seconds.

Some say the lighthouse is haunted. During the 1930s the New London Ledge keeper's wife ran away with the captain of one of the Block Island ferries that passed by the lighthouse almost every day. The distraught keeper pushed open the steel lantern door and jumped to his death on the rocks below. Later keepers claimed they heard strange noises and footsteps, found the lantern door open when they were sure they had closed and bolted it, and felt "cold spots" in certain rooms. Now that the lighthouse is automated, the New London Ledge ghost, if there is one, must be very lonely.

This unique structure can be seen from several vantage points on Ocean Beach on the south side of New London. Passengers on the Block Island Ferry, which operates from mid-June to Labor Day, enjoy a particularly fine view of the light. For ferry information call (203) 442–7891.

Built on submerged rocks, the New London Ledge Lighthouse looks entirely at odds with its surroundings. Some say the lighthouse is haunted.

OTHER CONNECTICUT LIGHTS
1805, 1824, 1826, 1840, 1868

Like its neighbor Rhode Island, Connecticut is a friend of the sea. The typically calm waters of Long Island Sound form a highway for ships. Its proximity to heavily traveled shipping channels helped make Connecticut a successful colony and, after the Revolution, a prosperous state. Not surprisingly, Connecticut has lots of lighthouses, many of them dating back nearly two centuries.

Among the oldest and best known of these is the New Haven Harbor Lighthouse, established in 1805. New Haven's first light tower was made of wood, but it was replaced by a more sturdy stone tower in 1840. Its light guided ships in and out of the New Haven Harbor until the lighthouse was decommissioned in 1877. Today it serves as the chief attraction of the city's Lighthouse Park.

The Stonington Harbor Lighthouse, built in 1824, first stood on Windmill Point. Erosion undercut the structure, and in 1840 the government had it torn down and rebuilt on the east side of the harbor. A thirty-five-foot stone tower with attached dwelling, this lighthouse was discontinued in 1889; but like the New Haven Harbor Lighthouse, it has miraculously survived the years. Today the Stonington Historical Society uses it as a museum.

Another lighthouse that has stood dark for nearly a century can be found on Sheffield Island in Norwalk. Established in 1826 and rebuilt in 1868, the gabled, two-story stone building served as a lighthouse until the turn of the century. Shortly after 1900 it was decommissioned. Restored and cared for by the Norwalk Seaport Association, the old lighthouse is now open to the public.

The octagonal stone tower of New Haven Harbor Lighthouse has stood since 1840. Out of service for more than a century, the old tower has miraculously survived the ravages of time and urban growth. (© William Kaufhold)

Its lens removed long ago, the stubby stone tower of Stonington Lighthouse (left) still stands. Resembling a small New England country church, the Sheffield Lighthouse (right) is another historical survivor. (© William Kaufhold)

For **New Haven Harbor** Lighthouse, take exit 50 off I–95 and follow Townsend Avenue (Route 337) south; then turn right onto Lighthouse Road. Lighthouse Park features not only the old lighthouse tower but also a nice beach.

For **Stonington Harbor Lighthouse** follow U.S. 1 east from New London to Stonington. Turn right on Water Street and follow it through historic Stonington Village to its end at the lighthouse. Located in the venerable structure is the Old Lighthouse Museum, open 11:00 a.m. to 4:30 p.m. daily (except Mondays) from May through October.

The **Sheffield Island Lighthouse** is located on a scenic island that also contains a noted wildlife refuge. Together the lighthouse and Stewart McKinney National Wildlife Refuge make the island well worth a visit. Passage to Sheffield Island is available from Hope Dock in Norwalk. Take exit 14 off I–95 and follow Fairfield Avenue and then Washington Street. Turn left on Water Street and look for the dock immediately on the right. For information on lighthouse cruise schedules and fares, call (203) 334–9166.

MONTAUK POINT LIGHT

Long Island, New York - 1797

The prominent bluff at the far eastern extremity of Long Island reminded early European settlers of the hump in a turtle's back, so they called the place Turtle Hill. But the unpretentious name belies the importance of this strategic point of land.

Long before the arrival of the white man, the first beacons burned on the hill known to Indians as "Womponamon." According to legend, leaders of the powerful Montauk tribe lit signal fires at the summit of the hill to call their chiefs and

A member of Montauk Point Lighthouse Association lowers Old Glory. The Association has helped save the lighthouse and operates a first-rate museum in its keeper's dwelling.

warriors to council. The vessels guided by these fires were dugout canoes carved from the trunks of large trees.

Some say the British also banked bright fires on the hill. During the Revolutionary War, several of King George's ships lay off Montauk Point in order to blockade Long Island Sound. The fires served these warships as beacons.

After the war, the new United States government recognized that it must follow the example of the British and the Indians before them. Such a significant and dangerous headland could not be left unmarked, and President George Washington himself ordered construction of a lighthouse on Montauk Point. It was to be an expensive project. Contractor John McComb of New York submitted a low bid of $22,300 to dig foundations, haul sandstone, and build the tower and two-story keeper's dwelling. At a time when lighthouses elsewhere were being built for as little as $2,000, this was a hefty price. Land for the light station had been purchased for only a little more than $250. But McComb gave the country its money's worth. He built the lighthouse like a fortress, with a foundation thirteen feet deep and walls seven feet thick at the base. As a consequence, the Montauk Point Lighthouse still stands after almost two centuries of blasting by Atlantic storms. McComb was also the contractor for a lighthouse erected in 1791 on Cape Henry in Virginia (see *Southern Lighthouses* by Bruce Roberts and Ray Jones; Globe Pequot Press), and the tower he built there, though unused for more than a century, stands to this day.

Generations of immigrants caught their first sight of America at Montauk Point,

Its light a welcome greeting to countless immigrants bound for New York, the Montauk Point Lighthouse was once as much a symbol of America as the Statue of Liberty.

and the lighthouse there became for many of them a symbol of the freedom and opportunity waiting for them in their new country. Like the Statue of Liberty, which also served for a while as a lighthouse, the Montauk Point Light reminds us of the vast migrations that filled up a continent and of the many nations that came together in America to form one nation. That the old light tower should fall is unthinkable; it would be as if someone chiseled the faces off the side of Mount Rushmore.

But only a few years ago, the unthinkable nearly happened. The elements have long threatened the destruction of the lighthouse, and the same ocean gales that, with all their fury, have never succeeded in blowing over the tower, have been slowly cutting away at the ground beneath its foundations. By the late 1960s, erosion had worn away more than 200 feet of the bank in front of the lighthouse and brought the structure within fifty feet of toppling into the sea. Unable to stop the ocean's seemingly inexorable advance, the Coast Guard prepared to abandon the station and build another lighthouse elsewhere. At this point, a remarkable New Yorker named Giorgina Reid came to the rescue.

Reid had invented a new way to stop erosion on hillsides and had even been granted a patent for her innovative technique. She called her method "reed-trench terracing" and had described it in a book with the title *How to Hold up a Bank.* Reid had noticed that nature uses a combination of sand, soil, and vegetable matter, such as dried reeds, to build up dunes and bluffs. She believed that with an assist from man—-and woman—the same combination of natural materials might halt the runaway erosion at Montauk Point and save the lighthouse. With Coast Guard permission she began the backbreaking task of digging trenches all over the eroded faces of Turtle Hill. Into these trenches she stuffed the withered stems of tall grasses and reeds. While resisting runoff and gullying, the trenches tended to catch and hold moisture which, in turn, gave soil-grabbing grasses and other plants a chance to grow. According to Coast Guard officials, the Reid (no play on words intended) prescription has succeeded, and her two-century-old patient is now out of danger.

Thanks to Reid's trenches, the Montauk Point Lighthouse continues to guide ships more than 190 years after its lamps first burned. Not all of the sailors who have seen the light have reached port safely, however. Storms have driven many vessels against the beaches near Montauk, usually with disastrous results. Some ships got permanently stuck in the sand, others broke in half and sank, and a few "melted like a lump of sugar" in the raging surf. More than a century ago, natives told a correspondent for *Harper's New Monthly* magazine about "how a ship was driven ashore one wild night . . . how brave men gathered to the rescue; how the crew, one after another dropped into the sea, some of them being saved from the jaws of the angry waves; of a mother washed ashore, dead, clasping a babe in her arms; the wild figures of the wreckers on that dark, stormy night of horrors, lit up by a great fire of drift-wood. . . ."

Ships are not the only wrecks found on the Montauk beaches. Whales occasionally end their days there as well. For reasons that are still not understood, whales sometimes beach themselves on the shores of Long Island and elsewhere. Unless they can be coaxed or winched back into the ocean, they die. Long Island settlers and, no doubt, the Indians before them, were quite familiar with the phenomenon of beached whales. The first pastor of the church at East Hampton, a few miles from Montauk, received as his salary "forty-five pounds annually, lands rate free, grain to be first ground at the mill every Monday, and one-fourth of the whales stranded on the beach."

For many decades, the lamps of the lighthouse at Montauk Point burned whale oil, though it was a commercial variety and was not taken from the unfortunate whales that happened onto nearby beaches. By the mid-1850s whalers had decimated the world's whale population. Seeing that it could no longer count on a regular supply of whale oil, the Lighthouse Service switched to lard oil as a fuel here and elsewhere. Later, many lighthouse lamps, including those at Montauk, burned kerosene.

This modern beacon replaced a first-order Fresnel lens at Montauk.

Follow Route 27 to Montauk Point State Park at the far eastern end of Long Island. If you could visit only one lighthouse in America, the Montauk Light would be a good choice. The museum in the old keeper's dwelling displays an outstanding collection of nautical and lighthouse artifacts, including several classic Fresnel lenses. The museum is well worth the small admission charge, which goes toward preservation of the Montauk Lighthouse.

ORIENT POINT LIGHT
Orient Point, New York - 1899

Just off the northeastern tip of Long Island, a deep but narrow passage called Plum Gut links several heavily trafficked bodies of water, including Long Island Sound and Gardiners Bay. Strong currents make navigating the Gut a tricky business. But a helmsman's chief concern is Oyster Pond Reef, a deadly ledge lurking just beneath the surface of the water and extending fully one-third of the way across the Gut.

To mark this unseen menace, in 1896 the Lighthouse Board approved construction of a caisson-type tower in the open water at the far end of the reef. The Orient Point Lighthouse took two years to build and was not operational until 1899. It cost $30,000, about six times the original estimate for the project. To protect the structure from high waves driven by gales, the builders piled hundreds of tons of broken stone around its base. Painted brown at the top and white at the bottom, the cast-iron tower was not particularly handsome and was soon given the nickname "Coffee Pot" by mariners who passed regularly through the Gut.

The station's first keeper was N. A. Anderson, a Norwegian immigrant. Keeper Anderson was married, but because his isolated light station was considered too small and dangerous for a woman, his wife lived in the town of Orient on Long Island. Anderson served for twenty years in the Coffee Pot at a salary of $50 a month.

Now unmanned and automated, the Orient Point Light guides maritime traffic with a white flash every five seconds. The tower stands sixty-four feet above the water, and its light can be seen for fifteen miles.

The lighthouse cannot be reached by land but can be seen from Orient Point, New York.

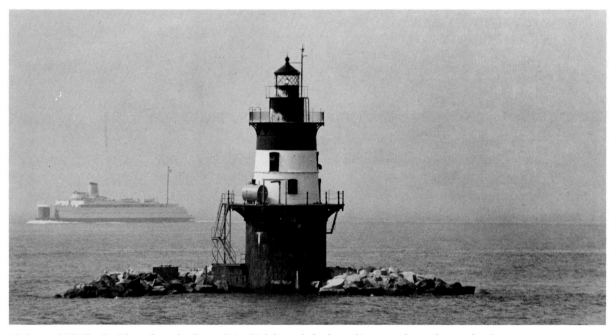

Nicknamed "Coffee Pot" by sailors, the Orient Point Lighthouse helps keep ships away from submerged rocks.

HORTON POINT LIGHT
Southold, New York - 1790, 1857

In 1757 during the French and Indian War, a young military officer from Virginia paused atop one of the high bluffs of Southold, New York, and gazed thoughtfully down onto Long Island Sound. He had come here to see firsthand a notorious stretch of coast known to locals and to the survivors of no few shipwrecks as "Dead Man's Cove." The Virginian told his companions that someday a lighthouse would be built on the very spot where he was standing. His name was George Washington, and many years later, in 1790, while serving as the nation's first president, he would commission the lighthouse himself.

In June 1990 the Horton Point Lighthouse celebrated the 200th anniversary of its commissioning. The event, attended by dignitaries and many "friends" of the old lighthouse, was doubly significant. On that same day the light was restored to active service after standing dark for fifty-eight years, the Coast Guard having decommissioned the lighthouse in 1933.

The Horton Point Lighthouse seen today was built on the bluffs during the mid-1850s. In June of 1857, almost exactly 100 years after Washington first visited the place, the whale-oil lamps were lit and the third-order Fresnel lamp began to throw light out over the sound.

President George Washinton commissioned the Horton Point Lighthouse in 1790. Washington first visited this site many years earlier while serving as an officer in the French and Indian War. (© William Kaufhold)

From 1903 to 1904, Stella Prince served as keeper of the Horton Point Lighthouse. Born and raised in the lighthouse itself, she was the daughter of an earlier keeper. Appointed by President Theodore Roosevelt, she was one of only a few women ever to receive official appointment as a lighthouse keeper.

From Route 25 or Route 48 in Southold, follow Horton Lane toward Long Island Sound. Turn right on Sound View Road and then left on Lighthouse Road. The Southold Historical Society operates a delightful nautical museum at the lighthouse. Hours are 11:30 A.M.–4:00 P.M. on Saturday and Sunday during summer months. For more specific information or for special tours, call (516) 765–3262.

FIRE ISLAND LIGHT
Fire Island, New York - 1826

In 1850 the *SS Elizabeth* struck the sandy shoals off the south coast of Long Island and sank almost within sight of the Fire Island Light station. Ironically, the ship's captain had been looking for the light when he hit the shoals. Many of the *Elizabeth*'s crew were drowned, and the disaster precipitated a public outcry. Mariners complained that the seventy-four-foot Fire Island tower, built in 1826, was far too short to accomplish its task of warning sailors away from the shoals.

Although Congress quickly appropriated money to rebuild the lighthouse and raise the height of the tower, nothing was done until construction began in 1857. By that time the Lighthouse Board had launched a major effort to revamp the nation's sadly deteriorated system of navigational lights. Some lighthouses were repointed and repaired while others were pulled down and replaced altogether. Lantern rooms all along the eastern seaboard received improved lamps and the marvelously effective Fresnel lenses made in Paris.

The plan for Fire Island included a new tower nearly twice as high as the original. When masons laid the last brick on the tower during the fall of 1858, it stood 180 feet above the ground. A steel circular staircase with 192 steps led to the lantern room. The low, sandy island gave the tower a boost of about seventeen feet, so the station's new Fresnel lens flashed its message to ships at sea from a point 168 feet above the water.

The Lighthouse Board long considered the Fire Island Light one of its most important light stations. Because of its flashing characteristic, the light is known affectionately to many as "Winking Woman."

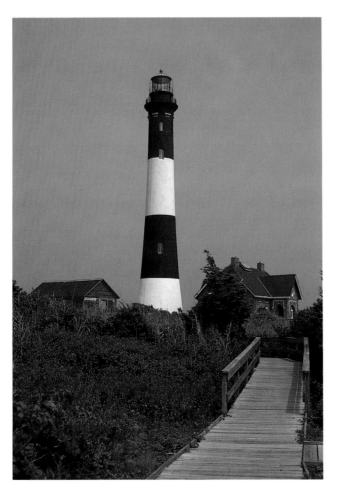

The light can be reached by road from West Islip or by ferry from Bay Shore. The light stands high above the low, sandy barrier island. Once on the island, just head toward the lighthouse; you can't miss it. The Fire Island Preservation Society has restored and relit the old 1858 lighthouse, installed an interpretive center in the living quarters, and established a foundation to maintain the station.

Decommissioned by the Coast Guard, Fire Island Lighthouse went dark in 1974. But it burns brightly again now, thanks to the efforts of a local preservation society.
(© William Kaufhold)

SANDY HOOK LIGHT
Sandy Hook, New Jersey - 1764

On the evening of June 11, 1764, a keeper trudged up the steps of the recently completed Sandy Hook Lighthouse and lit its oil lamps for the first time. Today, more than two-and-one-quarter centuries later, the light at the top of the old tower still burns each night. Although it was not America's first lighthouse—that honor

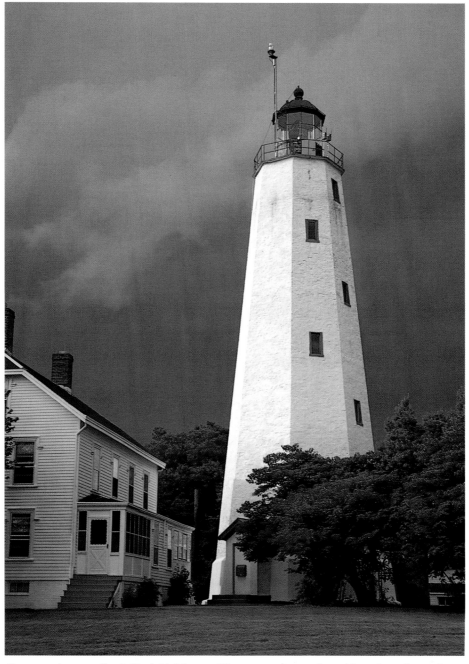

Storms gather over Sandy Hook Lighthouse. The octagonal tower has withstood weather and war since 1764. (© William Kaufhold)

goes to the Boston Light established in 1716 and destroyed by the British in 1779—it is the nation's oldest still standing and operating navigational aid.

Although located in New Jersey, the Sandy Hook Light was known for many years as the New York Lighthouse. Indeed, it was built and paid for by New Yorkers. Weary of losing commerce to better-marked harbors at Boston and elsewhere, a group of New York merchants petitioned their colonial council for a lighthouse. The New York Assembly then held a lottery to raise money and hired Isaac Conro to build a tower near the mouth of the Hudson. To defray the costs of maintenance and pay the keeper's salary, the Assembly levied a tax of twenty-two pence per ton on ships arriving at the Port of New York.

When completed, Conro's handiwork was described as follows: "The House is of an Octogan Figure, having eight equal sides; the Diameter of the Base 29 feet; and at the Top of the Wall 15 feet. The Lanthorn is 7 feet high; the Circumference 15 feet. The whole Constructure of the Lanthorn is Iron; the Top covered with Copper. There are 48 Oil Blazes. The Building from the Surface is Nine Stories; the whole from Bottom to Top 103 feet." The dimensions of the tower remain roughly the same today.

After the Revolution, the Sandy Hook Light precipitated a different sort of war. Since the lighthouse was located in New Jersey but owned by New York, the two states fell into a heated dispute over control of the station. The verbal and legal squabbling continued for years until the U.S. government finally put an end to the almost-comical conflict in 1789 by making the Sandy Hook station and other lighthouses a federal responsibility.

When the Lighthouse Board began its massive effort during the 1850s to rebuild and modernize America's outdated light stations, inspectors were sent to see if the Sandy Hook tower would need to be replaced. Their report to the board is a compliment to the work done by Conro almost a century earlier: "The tower at Sandy Hook main light was constructed in 1764 under royal charter, of rubble-stone, and is now in a good state of preservation. Neither leaks nor cracks were observed in it. The mortar appeared to be good, and it was stated that the annual repairs upon this tower amount to a smaller sum than in towers of any of the minor lights in the New York District."

The board did decide to replace the reflectors in the lantern with a third-order Fresnel lens. Its focal plane eighty-eight feet above the water, the old lens still guides ships into the New York Harbor with a fixed white light visible from about nineteen miles away.

Take Route 36 to Highlands Beach, enter Sandy Hook National Park, and follow the signs to the lighthouse. Still owned and maintained by the Coast Guard, the lighthouse can be approached for viewing. For current information call the Sandy Hook National Park at (908) 872–0115.

NAVESINK (TWIN LIGHTS) LIGHTS

Highlands, New Jersey - 1828, 1862

Among the most historic lighthouses anywhere in America are the twin rubble-stone towers atop the Navesink Highlands, just south of Sandy Hook. Navigational lights shined from this bold headland for almost two centuries, and uncounted thousands of mariners owe the safety of their ships and their very lives to the guidance these lights provided.

Rising some 200 feet above sea level, the highlands themselves have always served as a natural daymark. Long before the first lights were established here during the mid-1700s, the hills were observed and noted in the logs of European explorers who passed along what is now the northern New Jersey coast. One such adventurous navigator was Henry Hudson, who sailed his ship *Half-Moon* out of the misty waters off Sandy Hook Bay on September 2, 1609. Hudson and his crew saw a series of "high hills" rising from the mists. When the weather cleared enough for them to move in for a closer look, they discovered "a very good land to fall with and a pleasant land to see."

Many others also found these lands pleasant, as New Jersey and New York grew into prosperous colonies with bustling ports near the mouth of the Hudson River. To protect these ports from raids by enemy fleets, the colonists established an early-warning station at Navesink. Whenever a likely hostile fleet was sighted, a beacon was lighted to alert colonists and their militia as far away as New York City. Ironically, the first Navesink lighthouse was meant as a warning to landward folk rather than to ships and seamen.

A true navigational light is believed to have been in operation here as early as 1756. The light is mentioned in some documents dating to the Revolutionary War, but little else is known about it.

With American independence came a burgeoning of shipping traffic in and out of the Hudson. To help guide these ships, the Navesink Lighthouses were built in 1828. A matched pair of stone towers standing 320 feet apart placed the focal plane of the two lights more than 240 feet above sea level.

Government officials considered this to be among the best and most useful light stations in the country. In fact the

The fortresslike appearance of Navesink Lighthouse belies its peaceful mission. The twin-towered light station guided freighter traffic in and out of the Hudson River from 1828 until 1953. (Courtesy U.S. Coast Guard)

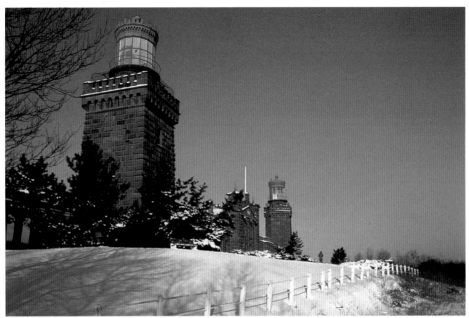

*The lighthouse is now part of a state historic site. (*Courtesy Twin Lights Historic Site)

Navesink station was considered so important to maritime commerce that the nation's first Fresnel lenses were installed in its towers. In 1838 Commodore Matthew Perry sailed for France, where he purchased a pair of the advanced prismatic lenses (one first order and one second order) and had them shipped to America. By 1841 the big Fresnels were shining powerfully from the twin Navesink towers.

There are several other firsts associated with the Navesink Lighthouses. They were the first in America to have lamps fueled by kerosene (1883). The first electrically powered seacoast light shined from the south tower beginning in 1898. (By that time an electric navigational light was already in use at the Statue of Liberty, but it served only as a harbor light.)

In 1899 the Navesink Highlands became the site of another "first" that had profound significance for navigation and for human progress. Employing a transmitter and mast located not far from the light station, Guglielmo Marconi conducted the first practical demonstration of his wireless telegraph. Using the air rather than a wire to carry the electronic dots and dashes, Marconi relayed the results of the America's Cup races off Sandy Hook.

The fortresslike brownstone towers seen today at Navesink date to 1861; they replaced the earlier structure at the beginning of the American Civil War. By 1898 the government no longer saw a need for two lights here and snuffed out the lamps in the north tower. The powerful south light, which could be seen from twenty-two miles at sea, served until 1953, when it, too, was discontinued. Today the station is part of Twin Lights Historic Site, administered by the New Jersey State Park Service.

To reach the Twin Lights Historic Site, take exit 117 off the Garden State Parkway and follow Highway 36 to Highlands and the museum parking lot. A small Fresnel lens can be seen at the museum, which features displays recounting the rich history of the station. Museum hours are from 10:00 a.m. until dusk daily. During the winter, the museum is closed on Mondays and Tuesdays.

BARNEGAT LIGHT

Long Beach Island, New Jersey - 1835

The man who built the first lighthouse on New Jersey's Barnegat Inlet was none other than Winslow Lewis, a key figure in the early history of the American lighthouse establishment. A retired sea captain, Lewis held a patent on the Argand lamp and parabolic reflector system used in many American lighthouses until the 1850s. A friend of Treasury Department Fifth Auditor and lighthouse czar Stephen Pleasonton, Lewis often won contracts to build and equip light stations.

Lewis's forty-five-foot Barnegat Inlet tower stood for only about twenty years before a Lighthouse Board inspector found it to be poorly constructed, in a

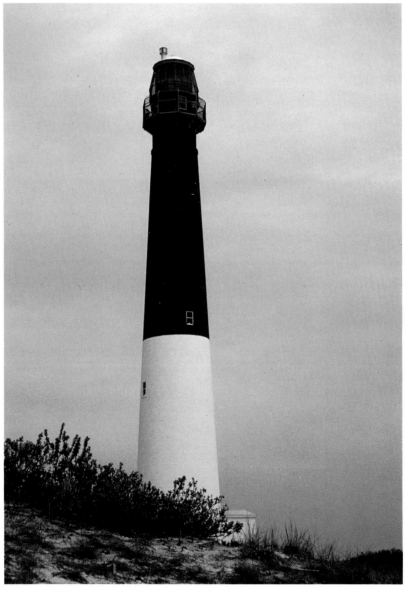

Barnegat Lighthouse waits for dark to project its beam and guide ships along New Jersey's sandy shores. (© William Kaufhold)

woeful state of disrepair, and hopelessly inadequate for service as a seacoast light. In truth, the board did not think much of Lewis's reflectors, either, and was busy replacing hundreds of them with the vastly more effective Fresnel lenses made by the French.

The inspector who gave the light its bad report was Lieutenant George Meade. The lieutenant found that Lewis had used decidedly inferior materials in the tower. Mortar crumbled from between bricks, and just below the lantern, a wall bulged out and seemed about to fall. Even if it were repaired, the stubby Lewis tower would serve as little more than an inlet light. Meade felt the station was strategically located and deserved a more powerful light with a range sufficient to guide ships at sea. He concluded that the board had little choice but to replace the collapsing structure with a much taller and better-built tower.

Meade's point of view got plenty of support from mariners. Almost from the moment it went into service in 1835, captains complained about the weakness of the light. Some said it was often "impossible to tell whether it is a ship's light or a lighthouse." Mail steamer Captain H. K. Davenport described the light as "indifferent."

Acting on Meade's advice, the board erected a soaring tower, its lantern room perched 163 feet above the water. Fitted with a first-order Fresnel lens, the tower exhibited its powerful new light for the first time on January 1, 1859, and the station entered a new era as a true seacoast light. The nation was about to enter a new era as well. Only a few years after his visit to Barnegat in 1855, lighthouse inspector Meade would serve his country in a very different and significant way. As General Meade, in 1863, he commanded the Army of the Potomac during the all-important battle of Gettysburg.

Take Route 72 to Long Beach Island and follow the signs to Barnegat Lighthouse State Park. Along the way, you'll pass through Surf City, North Beach, Harvey Cedars, and Loveladies. The lighthouse is open daily, Memorial Day to Labor Day, and weekends only in May, September, and October. Visitors may take a self-guided tour to the top of the light.

CAPE MAY LIGHT
Cape May Point, New Jersey - 1824, 1847, 1859

At 170 feet tall, the tower of the Cape May Lighthouse soars above the flat, sandy New Jersey coastline and the blue Atlantic beyond. Built in 1859, the distinctive white tower still guides shipping along the coast and into Delaware Bay. The enormous tower replaced two earlier structures dating to 1824 and 1847 respectively.

Exactly 199 steps lead from the ground floor to the lantern room. The focal plane of the extraordinary, 600,000-candle-power beacon is 165 feet above sea level.

While the lighthouse is still active, it has been automated; most of the outbuildings and keepers' dwellings are no longer in use. The keepers' houses are currently under restoration.

According to local tradition (and to rangers at Cape May Point State Park), the old lighthouse has a certain strong influence on young lovers. More than one couple have become engaged at the top of the tower.

The grand, white tower of Cape May Lighthouse soars 170 feet into the New Jersey skies. Built in 1859, the tall lighthouse has guided ships into Delaware Bay since before the Civil War. A smaller tower was built here in 1824. (© William Kaufhold)

Follow the Garden State Parkway south until it ends at Cape May. Take Route 109 South and then Lafayette Street almost to the Atlantic. Then turn right onto Sunset Boulevard and follow it to Lighthouse Avenue. Turn right and enter Cape May Point State Park. There is a small admission fee to the lighthouse. For current park hours and fees, call (609) 884–5404.

BIBLIOGRAPHY

Adams, William Henry Davenport. *Lighthouses and Lightships: A Descriptive and Historical Account of Their Mode of Construction and Organization.* New York: Scribner, 1870.

Adamson, Hans Christian. *Keepers of the Light.* New York: Greenberg, 1955.

Beaver, Patrick. *A History of Lighthouses.* Secaucus, N.J.: Citadel, 1972.

Caldwell, Bill. *Lighthouses of Maine.* Portland, Me.: Gannett Books, 1986.

Frost, Walter S., and Harold G. Simms. *The Lighthouses of Maine: A Guide for Photographers and Artists.* Frost and Simms, 1980.

Hamilton, Harlan. *Lights and Legends: A Historical Guide to Lighthouses of Long Island Sound, Fishers Island Sound and Block Island Sound.* Stamford, Ct.: Wescott Cove Publishing Co., 1987.

Holland, Francis Ross, Jr. *America's Lighthouses: Their Illustrated History Since 1716.* Brattleboro, Vt.: Stephen Greene Press, 1972.

Moe, Christine. *Lighthouses and Lightships.* Monticello, Ill.: Moe, 1979.

Putnam, George R. *Sentinel of the Coasts.* New York: Norton, 1937.

Rattray, Jeannette Edwards. *Perils of the Port of New York: Maritime Disaster from Sandy Hook to Execution Rocks.* New York: Dodd, Mead, 1973.

Scheina, Robert L. "The Evolution of the Lighthouse Tower." *In Lighthouses: Then and Now* (supplement to the U.S. Coast Guard Commandant's Bulletin).

Snow, Edward Rowe. *Famous Lighthouses of America.* New York: Dodd, Mead, 1955.

_____. *Famous New England Lighthouses.* Boston: Yankee Publishing, 1945.

Sterling. R. T. *Lighthouses of the Maine Coast.* Brattleboro, Vt.: Stephen Daye Press, 1935.

United States Coast Guard. *Historically Famous Lighthouses.* CG-232, 1986.

_____. *Chronology of Aids to Navigation and the Old Lighthouse Service.* CG-485, 1974.

Weiss, George. *The Lighthouse Service: Its History, Activity and Organization.* Baltimore: Johns Hopkins University, 1926.

Welch, Wally. *The Lighthouses of Massachusetts.* Apopka, Fl.: Lighthouse Publications, 1989.

_____. *The Lighthouses of Rhode Island.* Apopka, Fl.: Lighthouse Publications, 1987.

LIGHTHOUSE INDEX

ABOUT THE AUTHORS

BRUCE ROBERTS is a freelance photographer living in rural Virginia. He launched his wide-ranging career by working on newspapers in Tampa, Florida; Wilmington, Delaware; and Charlotte, North Carolina. Bruce served as director of photography and as senior photographer at *Southern Living* magazine for more than a decade. His award-winning photographs have also appeared in *Life, Sports Illustrated,* Time-Life Books, and many other magazines and books. Some of his photographs rest in the permanent collection of the Smithsonian Institution. Both the National and Georgia nature conservancies have reprinted Bruce's nature photography.

RAY JONES is publisher of Country Roads Press, located in Castine, a small town on the coast of Maine. He began his writing career working as a reporter for weekly newspapers in Texas. He has served as an editor for Time-Life Books, as founding editor of *Albuquerque Living* magazine, and as a senior editor and writing coach at *Southern Living* magazine. Ray grew up in Macon, Georgia, where he was inspired by the writing of Ernest Hemingway and William Faulkner, and worked his way through college as a disc jockey.

PHOTO INFORMATION

The best time to photograph lighthouses is at dusk: the edge between day and night. The soft light after the sun is below the horizon brings magic to color photos. The light in a tower appears brighter as the daylight fades; and as dusk comes on, a lighthouse is at its best. See pages 45, 49, 72, 77, 90, and 101 for examples.

To capture this effect, use a tripod and slower shutter speeds. The pictures in this book were taken on Fuji 100 daylight film on a Nikon 8008 camera using either a wide-angle or telephoto lens. The dusk photo of Rockland Breakwater Lighthouse on page 45 was taken with a 300-mm telephoto lens set at f 4.5, and the shutter was open for a full-second exposure. Look at the photo opposite on page 44, which was shot from a passing ferry in midmorning. There is a bit of mystery and mood at dusk that is not there during midday.

The photo of Pemaquid Point on page 49 was taken looking east just after the sunset. The orange light of the setting sun has been replaced by a softer light reflected off clouds in the western sky (behind the camera), but there was still enough light to shoot at a shutter speed about 1/10 of a second. You can tell how long the exposure was by looking at the movement in the waves. Longer exposures will blur waves and turn them into a foggy countenance, which also makes interesting pictures. On pages 45 and 77 the harsh orange light of sunset has also faded into a more interesting and soft magenta light.

The picture of the Cape Elizabeth Light on page 59 was taken before the sunset but after the sun was low enough to be softened by a summer haze on the horizon. The long shadow under the eve is the tip-off here. A 300-mm telephoto lens was used from a distance of about 100 yards to keep the vertical lines of the house looking straight—by not tilting the camera up. When a camera tilts up, it makes the vertical lines tilt inward and often makes a building look as if it were falling over backward; a wide-angle lens will aggravate this look. Another way to prevent this amateur look is to put something interesting in the foreground and hold the camera level; see the examples on pages 61 (Cape Neddick with small red building and fence), 90, and 103.

On page 90 the picture of Mystic Seaport Lighthouse was taken an hour after sunset, when all the color had faded from the sky and a deep blue night look fell on the film. Exposure here was about ten seconds (perhaps a bit longer on daylight Fuji film). Daylight film will almost always give this deep blue just before total darkness in the sky. The trick here is not to wait until total darkness—you must have a smidgen of light to make it work.

Many of the photos were taken from a Cessna 172 light plane because it has a window that can be opened. Don't hold the camera outside, as the airstream will pull it and blur your photos; keep the lens just inside. The high-wing Cessna is best for these aerial photos because the wing is above the photographer. Shutter speeds of 1/500 of a second prevent blur from the plane's speed. For this book a short, 105-mm telephoto was used. See photos on pages 14, 19, 23, 24, 25, 27, 33, 42, and 43.

Inside the lighthouse a 24-mm wide-angle lens was used; see pages 34 and 116. Lighthouses are grand subjects, but don't overlook a keeper's house. Sometimes the light will reflect in the window, and details and close-ups can produce totally unexpected pictures. See page 31.